Word Plays

Word Plays

Collected Writings on Politics and Culture

Robert Brustein

Transaction Publishers

Transaction Publishers is an imprint of the Taylor & Francis Group, an informa business

This book is printed on acid-free paper that meets the American National Standard for Permanence of Paper for Printed Library Materials.

ISBN: 978-1-4128-6504-3 (hardcover); 978-1-4128-6561-6 (paperback)
Printed in the United States of America

Library of Congress Cataloging-in-Publication Data

A catalog record for this book has been requested

Dedication

To all those who try to improve the theater, and to my beloved soul mate, Doreen, who does her best to improve me.

Contents

Acknowledgments

I wish to express my warm gratitude to all those who helped me with this book. First, my good friends, Gene Goodheart and Leslie Epstein—two, often insufficiently celebrated, Solons of our culture. Second, the always welcoming and indispensable *Huffington Post*. Third, Andrew McIntosh and Mary E. Curtis at Transaction Publishers. Fourth, Samuel French, which has published three of these short plays as part of the Boston Theatre Marathon series. And finally, Kate Snodgrass, producer of that series, to whom I offer deep thanks, with much love.

Introduction

This is my fourteenth book of collected articles, and probably my last. Approaching my ninetieth birthday as we ready for press in January 2017, I can, of course, attribute such a sober prediction to my advanced age. But it is also shadowed by the conclusion of Obama's last term. I have grown more and more convinced that this extraordinary man has, almost by himself alone, kept a lot of us from despair during the last eight years of this Republic.

But not quite. For at the same time that we were being led by one of the best-informed men in the history of the presidency, most of his advances were being blocked by one of the most recalcitrant opposition parties in the history of Congress.

And the beat goes on. The Republican-dominated Senate and House were elected by the same voters who are now seriously considering making Donald Trump the leader of what once was called "the free world." (n.b. Alas, that atrocious possibility became a grim reality as this book was going to press.) There have been other scary, rabble-rousing, proto-Fascist politicians in American history—Huey Long of Louisiana, for example, and George Wallace of Alabama. But while these men harbored presidential ambitions, they did not enjoy the support of a large number of the electorate. I can't imagine Donald Trump winning the presidency either. But the fact that he has gained so much support among the angry and the disenchanted is a frightening and virtually unprecedented development in our history.

What does a playwright and theater professor have to contribute to such a frightening political dilemma that media commentators and newspaper columnists have not already chewed over? Probably very little, except perhaps the capacity to look at the situation from a different perspective. I have never believed that culture and politics were separable categories. While always suspicious of propaganda plays, and highly alert to any sign of governmental intervention in the arts other than funding them, I have never wavered from a belief that culture and politics were tangential. The most productive example of such an alliance was the Federal Theatre under Hallie Flanagan Davis during its brief (four year) tenure in the 1930s. The most negative instance was the Un-American Activities Committee in the House under Martin Dies and, in the Senate, the Red-baiting McCarthy Committee.

Are Americans better protected today under our government than Egyptians under Morsi or Syrians under Assad or the great majority of rulers, including a few European ones, who close their prison doors on controversial artists? Of course we are. But that doesn't mean that we should weaken our vigilance regarding any constraints on artistic freedom, short of that shout of "fire" in that crowded room.

Most of us would rather be shouting "no more seats" in a crowded theater or "no more copies" in a congested bookstore. But while I have not always been able to fill a lot of seats with my plays, and rarely sold a lot of my books, I hope that this collection might help others achieve those elusive goals. Thank you for tolerating me over the past six decades.

I

Literary Word Plays

1

The Contemporary American Theater

Calling the American theater our most incisive record of American culture and society might seem like saying that the local strip joint is the best archive for the writings of Ludwig Wittgenstein. Even during the greatest periods of theater, serious critics have considered dramatic literature a lower form of activity. Sir Philip Sidney, who was William Shakespeare's contemporary, called the Elizabethan drama "a poor stepsister of the arts." Imagine how he would have scorned that ugly orphan known as the American theater! When the Harkness family offered Harvard, in the 1920s, a million dollars to build a stage for George Pierce Baker and his celebrated English 47 playwriting class, the university rejected the grant, saying, "We don't give degrees in butchering meat." (It may have been the first and only time in history that Harvard ever turned down a financial gift.) Baker took the money anyway and brought it to New Haven to form what would later be called the Yale School of Drama.

One of the first things the Puritans did after taking power in England in 1642 was to shut down the theaters. What an act of criticism! The clergyman John Harvard carried this legacy with him when he founded Harvard in 1638. It is not hard to understand the origins of religious contempt and academic scorn for the theater, a lot of which survives to the present day.

All through the previous century and up to the brink of World War I, our stage was dominated largely by melodrama, burlesque, vaudeville, and minstrel shows. The theater was hardly a place to examine pressing problems and urgent contemporary issues. It was a large bedroom where tired businessmen could snooze through soporific entertainment, totally indifferent to the vagaries of human character, much less to social, political, or metaphysical ideas.

It is true that Shakespeare, who embraced all imaginable dramatic concerns, remained a popular figure in the American theater, and not only on the New York stage. There were a number of national touring Shakespearean troupes on the road as well, bringing bowdlerized versions of *Hamlet* and *Othello* to Denver and St. Louis via overland trails. There is no doubt an apocryphal story that when *Othello* was being performed in a small Texas town, one Western witness got so riled up that he pulled out his six-gun and shot the actor playing Iago. (Killer and victim, the legend goes, were buried side by side with gravestones marked "Here lies the perfect actor" and "Here lies the perfect spectator.")

Around the turn of the century, one of these touring Shakespeare companies featured an actor named James O'Neill, Sr., who alternated the parts of Caesar and Brutus with the great Edwin Booth. If we are to believe his son, Eugene, writing about his father in *A Long Day's Journey into Night*, Booth highly praised James O'Neill's Othello, prophesying that he would become one of the finest Shakespearean actors of his day.

But James O'Neill went on to spend the greater part of his professional life as the star of an enormously successful, commercial touring version of Charles Fechter's *The Count of Monte Cristo*, forever regretting (if we are to believe Tyrone's melancholy comments in *A Long Day's Journey*) the prodigal waste of his talents. His son interpreted this as a more general American failing, not just of the theater but of the entire society.

There were occasional attempts at a serious national drama before Eugene O'Neill, a few desultory efforts to pinpoint areas of social and political unrest. Edward Sheldon, author of such insipid exercises as *Salvation Nell*, *Romance*, and *The Jest* had one eye cocked toward Europe and the other toward the movies, and Dion Boucicault contributed a sentimental glimpse into the evils of American slavery with *The Octoroon* in 1859. But Boucicault was not an American, he was an Irishman, and *The Octoroon* was more in the nature of a lament for a vanished patrician way of life than a protest against human bondage. (Indeed, it was an early example of the kind of mortgage melodrama that was to influence Chekhov's *The Cherry Orchard*.)

William Gillette wrote Civil War thrillers like *Secret Service*. Bronson Howard turned out Civil War melodramas like *Shenandoah* (1888). George L. Aiken dramatized Harriet Beecher Stowe's *Uncle Tom's Cabin*. And Steele Mackaye and William Dean Howells each tried his hand at parlor room plays, as did, more disappointingly, Henry James. With David Belasco (*The Girl of the Golden West*) and Clyde Fitch (*The City*), American drama turned its attention to the Gold Rush and drug abuse, while William Vaughn Moody in *The Great Divide* made some effort to contrast the values of the East and the West.

But the kind of social insight into American life and character familiar to readers of Whitman, Hawthorne, Emerson, Melville, Henry James, and other serious American writers was not to be found in the theater, not even in the awkward plays of Henry James himself who held the form in somewhat higher esteem than his contemporaries. It was unavailable, in fact, until the surprising appearance on the American stage of the Irish-American playwright Eugene O'Neill—the avant-garde son of a commercial star. And although his first efforts, the one-act sea plays he wrote for the Provincetown Playhouse on Cape Cod between 1916 and 1920, were not exactly focused on the more troubling questions of the day, it was not long before O'Neill embarked on something previously unheard of in the American theater, a critical confrontation with the values of his country, its moral stance, its social posture, its political policies—during that monolithic period the Luce organization would later call "The American Century."

After O'Neill, American drama would never again seem the same. Although commercial theater, in its Broadway manifestation, would continue to focus on entertainment, it would henceforth also give a place to more ambitious drama; and if this proved too strong for Broadway audiences, it could always find a welcome in the smaller theaters being created to house and encourage it, such as the Provincetown Playhouse and Cherry Lane Theatre in New York. American literary critics, like their predecessors throughout history, would continue to scorn American drama as an inferior species. But a new breed of critics with more scholarship, sensitivity, and skill would soon be writing about the form, demanding that the drama be allowed its rightful place in the creative pantheon.

And that did come about. Being the most communal and collective of the arts, including what Hamlet called "guilty creatures sitting at a play," theater always had the potential to catch the conscience of its audience. *Word Plays* will examine how, in the past hundred years, American dramatists, theaters, critics, and audiences finally began to embrace the cultural and political responsibilities of the stage.

Indeed, our drama would increasingly chronicle the growing pains and contortions of this century, as succeeding administrations in Washington were laboring to establish and consolidate our country as the most powerful nation on earth. War, the Depression, the development of labor unions, political agitation, Fascism, McCarthyism, the civil rights movement, psychedelic experimentation, racism, sexism, and trans-sexualism, these were to become the subjects of a previously scorned and discarded artistic form, now positioned not only to invent powerful stories about contemporary Americans, but also to provide unprecedented insight into the cultural history of the time.

Alienation

The 1920s represented O'Neill's decade on the American stage. Starting with a Pulitzer Prize for his first full-length play, *Beyond the Horizon* in 1920, this brooding, handsome playwright won every conceivable award, capped by the Nobel Prize, and created a succession of hits on Broadway that quickly established him as one of the leading dramatists in the world. His earlier one-act sea plays, produced between 1916 and 1920 in association with the Provincetown Players, though occasionally spiked with subtle references to the European war (e.g., the spy plot of *In the Zone*), were essentially character studies. But even these short works immediately signaled that an unusually serious temperament was occupying the American stage. Before long this dramatist would be writing annual, sometimes semi-annual, plays for Broadway, turning into a celebrity who dominated not only the theater pages but also the rotogravure sections of newspapers, with accounts of his European travels, love affairs, and divorces.

If O'Neill's earlier plays were unusually brief, his later work was to grow preternaturally long. An epic such as *Mourning Becomes Electra*, for example, took three days to perform.

Strange Interlude lasted seven hours. A country known for its gigantism had finally found a giant to match its size.

O'Neill's plays covered a wide spectrum of subjects—black colonialism in *The Emperor Jones* (1920); class conflict in *The Hairy Ape* (1922); prostitution in *Anna Christie* (1922); colonial imperialism in *Marco's Millions* (1923–25); miscegenation in *All God's Chillun Got Wings* (1924); marriage in *Welded* (1924); New England sexual repression in *Desire under the Elms* (1925); and rampant industrialization in *Dynamo* (1929). Some of these plays evoked the wrath of the civic authorities, particularly *All God's Chillun Got Wings*, which was banned in London, San Francisco, and, needless to say, the city of Boston, because of its heterodox racial attitudes. *Desire under the Elms*, characterized by advanced *sexual* behavior, drew an injunction from the New York District Attorney, once again banned in Boston and England, and shuttered in Los Angeles after the cast got arrested.

Almost all of these plays were marked not just by forbidden subject matter but also by formal innovation, whether in the use of masks, or doppelgangers, or expressionism, or soliloquies and asides. O'Neill, virtually alone among his contemporaries, was highly indebted to European influences, especially to their structural innovations. He found Strindberg particularly congenial, drawn to the Swedish playwright because of his tragic intensity, relentless experimentation, and mental instability. He was also impressed by the way the Italian dramatist Pirandello shattered illusion, by the Expressionism of the Germans Toller and Kaiser, and in his final years by the "Kodak realism" of the Norwegian Henrik Ibsen. These influences were not just formal. Like O'Neill, all of these playwrights were in revolt against the bourgeois materialism of their times, drawn to Bohemian freedom, and alienated by the coarse greed and ambition of what Ibsen scornfully called "the pillars of society."

Despite his cosmopolitanism, however, O'Neill was also American to the core, especially in his sorrowful characterization of his country and his culture as primitive and provincial. The nation's great intellectual gadflies, H. L. Mencken and George Jean Nathan, encouraged O'Neill to deal with some of the very issues being treated in American novels and poetry, not to mention in American historical writing and the social sciences. Although O'Neill (despite an early flirtation with anarchism) was never a Communist Party member, his chief subject in the 1920s was the corruption of capitalism, which he dramatized as a battle between the idealist and the philistine, or, as he would put it in *The Great God Brown*, between the poet and the businessman.

O'Neill's revulsion over American philistinism and provincialism reflected the American flight from the village animating so many writers of the time, Hemingway, Fitzgerald, T. S. Eliot, and Sinclair Lewis among them, a flight not only spiritual but geographical, often leading to permanent or temporary exile abroad. A foreign war undertaken for the purpose of "making the world safe for Democracy" had left many young Americans dead on the battlefield, and democratic society just as insecure as ever. It had also exposed many Americans to the more cosmopolitan and sophisticated European culture and to the possibility of a more various and cultivated existence than Babbitt had been enjoying on Main Street. Hemingway escaped provincial America partly through his interest in bullfighting and African safaris. Fitzgerald exulted in the French Riviera and the ski slopes of Gstaad. T. S. Eliot became an expatriate in England, writing in the tradition of the English religious poets. Ezra Pound moved to Italy and became a Fascist.

In the theater, O'Neill was the leader of this cosmopolitan movement, but he was hardly alone in his critique of American morals and manners. His first tentative efforts would soon be followed by serious plays from Sidney Howard, rejecting the Puritan idea that marital adultery was an unforgivable sin in *They Knew What They Wanted* (written in 1925 but later musicalized in 1956 as *The Most Happy Fella*); from Maxwell Anderson with a series of blank verse plays, in imitation of the Elizabethan period, such as *Elizabeth the Queen* (1930) and *Mary of Scotland* (1933), as well as an antiwar play called *What Price Glory?* (1924), and a play about Sacco and Vanzetti called *Winterset* (1936); from Elmer Rice with a play based on the Expressionist techniques of Kaiser and Toller called *The Adding Machine* (1923), about the alienation of the worker and the mechanization of life in the industrial age. (Sophie Treadwell produced a similar exercise with *Machinal* in 1928.)

In short, American theater in the 1920s, under the leadership of O'Neill, was embarking on a mighty effort to establish itself as a serious, sophisticated art form, equal in risk-taking, experimentation, and intelligence to anything found on European stages, and rivaling such American novels as Hemingway's *The Sun Also Rises* and Fitzgerald's *The Great Gatsby* as platforms for serious ideas. And very quickly, this theater grew accustomed to criticizing (for their avarice, provincialism, religious bigotry, and Babbitry) the very audiences on whom it was dependent for its survival.

Revolt

After writing *Ah Wilderness!* and *Days Without End* in 1933, O'Neill did not give up theater, but he did withdraw from public life, refusing to let any of his plays be staged until well into the 1940s. Among these delayed productions were two pinnacles of his achievement, *The Iceman Cometh* (written in 1939, but not performed until 1946) and *A Long Day's Journey into Night* (written in 1941, but not performed until after his death in 1957). A similar fastidiousness was to delay his penetrating historical studies of America, *A Touch of the Poet*, written in 1942, but not performed until 1958, and *More Stately Mansions*, left unfinished and unperformed until 1967, both contributions to his projected nine-play cycle of American life. Each in its own way was deeply autobiographical, each represented deep probes into family and community, and each had historical dimensions. But each of them also dramatized O'Neill's conviction that America was a gigantic failure which had utterly botched its earlier promise.

O'Neill had rarely been an overtly political playwright. But partly because of his long self-enforced silence in the 1930s and largely as a result of the Depression's oppressive economic climate, the American stage was now being taken over by more politically radical artists, chiefly Clifford Odets, Albert Maltz, Lillian Hellman, and John Howard Lawson. The Great Depression of 1929 had created a huge dust bowl, plunging the country into despair and privation for the next twelve years. Nazism and Fascism had triumphed in Germany and Italy in the 1920s and 1930s, a civil war was erupting in Spain in 1936, and a second World War, far more toxic than the first, was preparing to break out at the end of the decade. No wonder that our theater, like our society, was experiencing a powerful upsurge in protest and social consciousness. Many American playwrights of the time had either joined the Communist Party, or become Socialists, Trotskyites, or some other variant of revolutionary Marxism. The most scorned literary figures were not conservatives or neo-conservatives, as they are today, but rather the much-ridiculed left-liberals personified by such paralyzed and ineffectual dramatic characters as Alan Squier in Robert Sherwood's *The Petrified Forest* (1936), a play about a liberal too passive to resist political evil.

Odets, who had developed a staccato style akin to blues and jazz, was doubtless the theatrical icon of this period, and such plays of his as *Waiting for Lefty* and *Awake and Sing* usually concluded less with some form of plot resolution than with ringing revolutionary speeches, either calls to strike or to overthrow the system. Paul Green's *Johnny Johnson*, a musical piece written in 1937 with the German expatriate and former Brecht collaborator Kurt Weill, vainly tried to promote peace in a world increasingly prone to violence. In *Dead End* (1935), Sidney Kingsley wrote about the deteriorating conditions of the metropolis.

As important as these dynamic new playwrights were, the vital new stages that produced them, such as the Group Theatre in New York and the Federal Theatre Project, which initiated work all over the country, were indispensable. The Federal Theatre was the more visionary of the two in that its leader, Hallie Flanagan Davis, was devoted to a national theater that was nonprofit in its structure, decentralized in its geography, ethnic in its scope, and designed to provide employment for the various unemployed theatre people in the land.

The Group Theatre was conceived more as a select artistic collective trained in the Stanislavski acting system (featuring such already well-known actors as Franchot Tone, Stella and Luther Adler, and Frances Farmer, along with such budding artists as Lee J. Cobb, Elia Kazan, and John Garfield). Despite its serious ambitions, however, the Group, lacking the subsidies of the Federal Theatre, was forced to operate under the pressures of the Broadway commercial system, which accounted for the shortness of its life (nine seasons). And although the Federal Theatre was created by a government agency (the WPA), its four-season life was to prove even shorter.

The leader of the Group Theatre, Harold Clurman, was essentially a left-liberal with a passion against injustice but with no interest at all in Communist solutions. Clurman's wife, Stella Adler, reputedly went on a protest march, wearing a mink coat and carrying a poodle. The leader of the Federal Theatre, Hallie Flanagan, was equally indifferent to the Communist Party. But there were unquestionably party members in each of those theaters, along with secret Communist cells, which soon attracted the attention of Martin Dies and the House Un-American Activities Committee.

Sniffing out Red influences (along with potential headlines), the committee put an end to the extraordinary experiment of the Federal Theatre after hasty hearings in which Flanagan was barely allowed to make her statement. Asked whether Christopher Marlowe was a Communist, she replied, "Put it in the record that he was the greatest dramatist in the period of Shakespeare." Chairman Dies finally had to get her removed from the committee room. "We don't want you back," he said. "You're a tough customer and we're all worn out."

Hallie was not, however, averse to didactic plays and even helped to write some herself for the Federal Theatre, among them such Living Newspaper exercises as *One-Third of a Nation* and *Triple-A Plowed Under*. But she had no use for propaganda works promulgating a single political cause, and while Federal Theatre productions were often activist they were rarely Communist. Neither this history nor her appearance before the House Un-American Activities Committee could prevent the Federal Theatre from being plowed under, especially with the New Deal now forced to cope with more important issues than the country's theatrical tastes. By a vote of 373 to 21, the House passed the Relief Bill for 1939–40 calling for sweeping changes in the WPA program, including drastic cuts in arts funding and the imposition of loyalty oaths designed to get rid of radicals. Sound familiar?

Of course, the Federal Theatre was not entirely free of political influences. Even some of its children's plays had Communist overtones.

Indeed, its major classical unit, run by Orson Welles and John Houseman, was also producing plays with a political spin, including a *Julius Caesar* set in Mussolini's black-shirt Italy, and a Voodoo *Macbeth* that provided African-American actors with their earliest opportunities to perform on the commercial stage. This unit was soon to break off from the Federal Theatre Project and become the independent Mercury Theatre, after the cancellation of one of its productions, Marc Blitzstein's anti-capitalist *The Cradle Will Rock*. (The whole event would later be dramatized in Tim Robbins' movie *Cradle Will Rock* with Cherry Jones playing Hallie Flanagan.)

Like its model, the Brecht-Weill *Threepenny Opera* (also scorned during its premiere on Broadway, though a great success in the 1950s), the politics and style of the agitprop *Cradle Will Rock* would influence many musicals to come. Even commercial musical vehicles such as Gershwin's *Of Thee I Sing* (1931), with its satire on presidential campaigns, would carry political luggage. The interesting thing about the 1930s is that while the theaters were comparatively radical, the audiences were essentially liberal. (The same thing characterized Hollywood in the 1930s.) That is why artists and audiences could find common ground on such subjects as the Spanish Civil War, the evils of Nazism, the rise of unemployment, and the viciousness of lynch mobs in the South without having to agree on a common solution. In short, they shared a sentiment without sharing an ideology, remaining uneasy allies in a conflict with an easily recognized enemy. Only when that enemy was perceived to be within as well as without, wearing a Communist face, was this political alliance broken.

If the Federal Theatre was suffering from incursions by Washington politicians, the Group Theatre was also vulnerable to Hollywood producers. One after the other its membership was lured (or lured back) to the movies, with

John Garfield (born Julius Garfinkle) becoming, after Paul Muni (born Frederich Meshilem Meier Weisenfreund), one of Hollywood's earliest ethnic matinee idols. However erratically, movies were beginning to realize their potential as a serious art form (though theater people, such as George S. Kaufman in *Once in a Lifetime*, would continue to scorn the system as fit only for popcorn eaters).

As for the commercial theater, it would always be available for anything that drew audiences, even if this happened to be a revolutionary play. If the radical Odets could be produced on Broadway, then so could Lillian Hellman, particularly with such subtle probes into the corruptions of capitalism as *The Little Foxes* (1939) and *Another Part of the Forest* (1948). Anti-Nazi plays were proving even more popular, especially after Britain entered the war in 1939 and the United States followed two years after. This was a decade in which the enemy lines were clearly drawn, and (until the formation of the Nazi–Soviet pact in 1939) Uncle Joe Stalin was a friendly, twinkling guest at the American table.

Patriotism

The 1940s corresponded with World War II, the end of the Depression, and an understandably flag-waving American mood. Apart from such anti-Nazi plays as Lillian Hellman's *Watch on the Rhine* (1941), Robert Sherwood's *There Shall Be No Night* (1940), and Maxwell Anderson's *The Eve of Saint Mark* (1944), this theatrically dim decade was characterized by such paeans to homey small town values as Thornton Wilder's *Our Town* (1940) and to such exertions of audience flattery as William Saroyan's *The Beautiful People* (1941). Inspired by Gertrude Stein's *The Making of Americans* (just as *The Skin of Our Teeth* owed a debt to Joyce's *Finnegans Wake*), *Our Town* nevertheless resided right in the center of Middle America, celebrating the domestic and patriotic values of a

New England village that seemed to be entirely without Jews, ethnics, or blacks. As a result, it proved to be the archetypal anti-Bohemian play, adored by mom and dad, and ideally suited for high-school senior shows. Even Wilder's considerably more experimental play *The Skin of Our Teeth* (1943), a whimsical look at the history of the world from Adam and Eve to the Apocalypse, took a comparatively optimistic and folksy view of American mores.

This was the period when the musicals of Rodgers and Hammerstein were becoming Broadway and Hollywood favorites. The sun-drenched meadows of *Oklahoma*, the hair-washed patriotism of *South Pacific*, and the Swiss yodeling of the Trapp Family singers in *The Sound of Music* were located in an entirely different province than the edgy, sophisticated world of Cole Porter, George Gershwin, and Rodgers himself when he was collaborating with Lorenz Hart. Urbanites who week-ended in Bucks Country and summered in East Hampton were celebrating the corn-fed values of rural America and the patriotic values of a nation at war. In fact, the theater work of the entire decade existed in almost self-conscious contrast to the alienated revolt of the 1920s and the radical protests of the 1930s.

Those Federal Theatre and Group Theatre artists who weren't living in Hollywood (like the Group's Franchot Tone, newly married to Joan Crawford) were now starting acting schools. With political activism in a state of narcosis as a result of domestic and foreign pressures, theater artists were becoming more engrossed with the weaknesses of their profession than with the failings of their country. Such Group Theatre alumni as Cheryl Crawford, Elia Kazan, and Bobby Lewis jump-started the Actors Studio, until their busy careers forced them to hand over the reins to Lee Strasberg.

Stella Adler, who had gone to Paris to complain that Stanislavsky had destroyed her love of acting, was told by the

Russian master that Strasberg was seriously misreading his system. She thereupon founded the Stella Adler Studio to reestablish the true Stanislavsky legacy, while Group alumni Bobby Lewis and Sanford Meisner each began corrective acting programs of their own. If the American actor could not find serious expression on a commercial stage grown lax, torpid, and irrelevant, he or she could at least find dignity doing scenes from great plays in acting studios. Except for a handful of serious works produced toward the end of the decade, when Arthur Miller wrote *All My Sons* (1947) and *Death of a Salesman* (1949), and Tennessee Williams wrote *The Glass Menagerie* (1945) and *A Streetcar Named Desire* (1947), the 1940s represented a period of good will, optimism, and artistic fatuity.

But this was also the decade that witnessed the Soviet Union's evolution from a wartime ally into an implacable enemy, when the Iron Curtain came down and the Cold War began to freeze relations among former allies. Many past American Communists had left the party after the Hitler–Stalin pact. Some, notably Lillian Hellman, continued to be Stalinist apologists, both in their theatrical work and in their public statements. This would lead to some celebrated breaks between old friends, most notably Hellman's quarrels with Mary McCarthy and later with Lionel and Diana Trilling, and the famous falling-out between Elia Kazan and Arthur Miller, while the same Congressional committees that had killed the Federal Theatre in the 1930s would retool to investigate the politics of the whole entertainment industry. Meanwhile, the Alger Hiss case, initiated in 1948 when Whittaker Chambers accused this well-respected American statesman (alas, correctly) of being a mole for the Soviet Union, would color not only liberal politics but also theatre relationships and attitudes throughout the next decade.

Whereas the 1920s and the 1930s were characterized by alienation and protest, the 1940s and 1950s were largely a celebration of "Our Country and Our Culture," to invoke the title of a notorious *Partisan Review* symposium. Formerly disaffected artists and intellectuals were being absorbed into the larger society, finding well-paying jobs in universities, on the staffs of large newspapers and magazines, and in major publishing houses, which, for a while, had the affect of stifling dissent and chilling diversity. It was later to develop into a movement called "Neo-Conservatism."

Conformity

The 1950s was the period of the Cold War, anti-Communism, McCarthyism, and, later, the Korean War. Brown versus the Board of Education signaled the beginning of a simmering crisis over civil rights and integration in America. Pioneering erotic books by Henry Miller, published abroad and smuggled into the country, were opening new avenues of subject matter for the likes of Norman Mailer and James Baldwin. In the theater, Arthur Miller and Tennessee Williams, having already established their artistic credentials with such plays as *The Glass Menagerie*, *All My Sons*, *A Streetcar Named Desire*, and *Death of a Salesman*, were now the idols of the 1950s, forming, with William Inge, a triumvirate that was shaking American theater awake after a long slumber.

The chief source of actors and directors for these playwrights continued to be the Actors Studio—not yet a producing unit (indeed, not to become one until the 1960s) so much as a conservatory promoting a particular style of acting. This style was best embodied by one man—Marlon Brando—with a host of imitators, including James Dean, Warren Beatty, Ben Gazzara, Paul Newman, Steve McQueen, among others. Like Dean, ironically, Brando had spent very little time in the Studio and (again like Dean) had little use for Strasberg, who nonetheless took credit for their success. (Brando always credited his teacher, Stella Adler.)

Still, the Studio style, with its emphasis on internal truth, was modeled to a large extent on Brando's playing of Williams' Stanley Kowalski—simultaneously uneducated and sensitive, explosive and repressed. Where the American stage hero used to feature a speaker, protesting—like Ralphie in *Awake and Sing*—the inequities of the system, it now preferred a grunter and a stammerer, who broke into violence, like Melville's Billy Budd, whenever unable to articulate his feelings.

Williams had designed the conflict between Blanche and Stanley in *Streetcar* as a reworking of the traditional American struggle, first explored on stage by O'Neill, between the artist and the philistine. (Indeed, Stanley may be Williams' later reworking of the hapless Yank in O'Neill's *Hairy Ape*.) In the sensitive playing of Marlon Brando, however, the ethnic Stanley sometimes seemed more delicate than the aristocratic Blanche. (When Anthony Quinn replaced Brando in the role, the balance was restored at a loss of some of the character's dynamism.) As for Inge, each of his central characters, however vigorous and masculine on the surface, was invariably reduced by play's end to a childlike state in the arms of a surrogate mother. In *Come Back, Little Sheba* (1950), *Picnic* (1953), and *The Dark at the Top of the Stairs* (1957), the muscle-flexing hero is forced to admit his fears and return to the safety of the hearth.

The Actors Studio acting style was perfectly suited to the simmering, neurotic, emotionally unstable, and essentially asocial characters of Williams and Inge, primarily because they had little political to say, though Williams did write one early play (*Not about Nightingales*) about cruel prison conditions, and quite a few about how sexual freedom threatened the bigoted Southern mindset (*Orpheus Descending*, *Sweet Bird of Youth*, and *Cat on a Hot Tin Roof*).

The vestigial political interests of Arthur Miller, on the other hand, especially in such earlier plays as *All My Sons*, which pointed a finger at war profiteers, and *Death of a Salesman*, indicting America's indifference to "the common man," required more eloquent actors of the kind previously associated with the Group (Lee J. Cobb) or the Yiddish Theatre (Paul Muni)—both of whom were among the many eloquent artists who played Willy Loman. But despite their variations in style or politics, Miller, Williams, and Inge all found their directorial inspiration in a single highly influential figure, a Group Theatre graduate and America's leading stage and film *auteur*, Elia Kazan. It was Kazan who had directed Miller's *All My Sons* and *Death of a Salesman*, Williams' *Streetcar Named Desire* and *Cat On a Hot Tin Roof*, and Inge's *The Dark at the Top of the Stairs*, along with a score of top-flight films (*Viva Zapata, On the Waterfront*, and *Splendor in the Grass*)—that is until, a former Communist Party member himself, he named the names of fellow party members to the House Un-American Activities Committee and was quickly toppled from his place at the pinnacle of the American theater.

Naming names was the activity that caused the greatest tumult in the American theater of that time. Some former party members testified before HUAC (and McCarthy) out of an honest conviction that Communism was undermining American democracy. Others testified in order to preserve their lucrative Hollywood contracts. Yes, there were blacklists such as Red Channels available to employers that could keep a screenwriter from working except under an assumed name. But blacklists affected only Hollywood and television employment. Very few artists were ever banned from the American stage as a result of political beliefs.

As a result of Kazan's testimony, Miller, along with a number of others who had defied HUAC, publicly broke with him. Miller wrote a play—*The Crucible* (1953)—about the inexcusable act of naming names, which he identified with witch-hunting. Kazan and Budd Schulberg made a movie—*On the Waterfront* (1954)—about the absolute necessity of naming names, which they associated with patriotism. Appearing before the committee with his new wife (Marilyn Monroe) on his arm, Miller was given a prison sentence for contempt of Congress, later overturned. (Chairman Dies himself had offered to suspend Miller's sentence if he could take his photograph with Marilyn—Miller refused.) Miller retained his reputation and the respect of the theater community, while Kazan advanced his film career at the cost of becoming a theater pariah. Years later, when he received an Academy Award for lifetime achievement in 1999, half the audience refused to applaud, and many booed.

In the Eisenhower 1950s, even the most political writers seemed to have lost their voices, and plenty of the old revolutionaries were expressing their discontents not in union halls or Communist cells but on psychiatrists' couches. Yes, there was a lot of vocal opposition to McCarthy—after all, the theater world was almost entirely liberal or leftwing—and a few stirring testimonies in the halls of Congress (most notably Lillian Hellman's "I cannot and will not cut my conscience to fit this year's fashions" speech) where a large number of people in the entertainment industry were being forced to defend themselves against charges of Communism, and where some of them, like the Hollywood Ten, were even being imprisoned for contempt of Congress. (These proceedings would later be dramatized in 1972 in Eric Bentley's *Are You Now or Have You Ever Been. . . .*) Such hearings were a continued reflection of Congressional fear of the erotic and political side of the creative instinct, the same fear that earlier killed the Federal Theatre and years later would emasculate the National Endowment for the Arts.

On the international front, few American plays or films were focusing on the scary hostilities that had broken out in the Far East between North and South Korea over a border (or parallel) dispute, a conflict that first drew the United States, then Communist China, into the fray, and was now threatening to erupt into a third world war. Even Arthur Miller, the one major activist left in American theater, seemed to ignore the Korean conflict. Instead, he began writing mostly domestic plays (*A View from the Bridge*, *The Price*) often with hidden themes about the evils of informing, and when he tried to indict modern McCarthyism in *The Crucible*, he chose to set the action in seventeenth-century Salem during the witch-hunting craze—an analogy that weakened his theme.

The problem was that Miller's lingering radicalism (like that of other vestigial leftists) no longer grew out of an ideology, which may be why the most famous sentence in *Death of a Salesman*—"Attention must be paid"—has no subject. Who must pay attention? The federal government? The Salvation Army? The American Psychiatric Society? The 1930s thought it knew the answer. If the 1950s knew, it kept that secret to itself.

These bland Eisenhower years saw the appearance of musicals such as the Bernstein–Laurents–Sondheim *West Side Story* (1957), with its *Romeo and Juliet* love story set against the background of ethnic gang warfare in Manhattan. The decade also produced *Gypsy* (1959), an Arthur Laurents' piece influenced by the mother figures in Williams and Inge, with a score by Jule Styne and lyrics by Stephen Sondheim. In its new effort to achieve the stature of a serious Broadway play, the Broadway musical remained torn between politics and entertainment. Indeed, the longest running musical of the 1950s was the Lerner–Loewe *My Fair Lady* (1956), an adaptation of a Shaw comedy about class-influenced language differences among the English. Perhaps the popularity of *My*

Fair Lady in this decade was due, apart from the fact that it was a beautifully crafted work, to having absolutely nothing whatever to do with American character and society. For the most part, this escapist dysfunction on the part of Broadway, as compared with the unrelenting artistic commitment of off-Broadway to major issues, was to cause some of the biggest cultural chasms of the time, especially after the appearance of Beckett, Ionesco, Pinter, Durrenmatt, Fugard, and other serious foreign playwrights on the serious American stage.

Psychedelia

In the 1960s, America was preparing to awaken from that long drugged sleep called the Eisenhower age and rub away the accumulated rheum of those eight drowsy years. The end of this national lethargy was signaled by a rush of radical dissent and artistic ferment—often stimulated by other kinds of drugs. Lenny Bruce was electrifying nightclub audiences with language never before heard in stand-up acts. Kenneth Tynan's *Oh! Calcutta* was exposing Broadway audiences to human body parts previously never seen on stage, even in burlesque shows. (So did *Hair* when the production moved to Broadway and Tom O'Horgan added full frontal nudity.) In the serious theater, starting with the advent of Edward Albee, the hoarse voice of the angry and the alienated was once again being heard, first in *The Zoo Story* (where the old theme of the artist vs. the philistine was being translated into the hipster vs. the square) and then in that epic marital spat called *Who's Afraid of Virginia Woolf?* But Albee was hardly the only critic of straight middle-class society. With the rise off-Broadway of the influential Living Theatre during this period, directed by Julian Beck and Judith Malina, such assaults on the audience as Jack Gelber's heroin-soaked *The Connection* (1959), whose drugged-out characters followed the spectators out of the theater and into the lobby, and Kenneth H. Brown's ear-shattering indictment of the Marine Corps prison system, *The Brig* (1963), divided audiences and critics into warring camps. After being savaged by the mainstream press, for example, *The Connection* won the praise of a number of intellectuals in the little magazines (it was, e.g., the exemplary subject of the very first review I wrote for *The New Republic* toward the end of 1959). As a result, it not only survived its bad mainstream notices but also enjoyed a record-breaking run. Aside from demonstrating the revitalization of off- and off-off-Broadway theater, these productions initiated a culture war between the daily and weekly press that was to help give new impetus to the minority theater movement.

In 1956, for example, the most respected theater reviewer for the daily newspapers, Walter Kerr of the New York *Herald Tribune*, could confidently patronize the Broadway production of *Waiting for Godot* as some kind of precious highbrow pratfall, out of touch "with the minds and the hearts of the folk out front." After *The Connection* in 1959, he was never again to seem as certain that he was writing for a consensus. Nor was Howard Taubman, then drama critic for the *New York Times*, who never wrote with the confidence that once marked the reviews of Brooks Atkinson. In the minority theater, at least, the centers of influence were shifting, and artists and intellectuals for the first time were beginning to hope that some day they might have a theater, too. *The Connection* may have been the first battlefield on which these wars were fought, but it was hardly the last. Harold Clurman of *The Nation*, Jerry Tallmer of *The Village Voice*, and even Donald Malcolm of *The New Yorker* joined other minority critics in turning that production into a *cause celebre* with an international reputation. When the *Times* and the *Tribune* later savaged Jonathan Miller's delicate treatment of Robert Lowell's *The Old Glory* at the American Place Theatre, I whimsically proposed a pact to their reviewers—offering to stop covering musicals and melodramas if they would give up covering serious plays.

While we critics were swatting away at each other, Broadway and off-Broadway seemed to be forming an alliance in the newly formed Lincoln Center company, with classics being offered along with new American plays by a resident company of actors. Although run by two Broadway figures—Elia Kazan and Robert Whitehead—Lincoln Center represented a kind of recognition on the part of the commercial theater that there was a theatrical world elsewhere. Lincoln Center was also the locus for an unexpected reunion between Miller and Kazan during its first season with Miller's *After the Fall* (1964). Although this play described Kazan's political defection from the Left with his HUAC testimony and followed Miller's marriage to Kazan's one-time lover Marilyn Monroe, the production was staged by none other than the villain of the piece, Kazan himself. Despite the titillating, self-exonerating way it mixed fiction and fact from the lives of its playwright and director, the play was an artistic failure that belonged more to the world of tabloid gossip (though this has its delicious side) than to theatrical anthologies.

Miller's next play for Lincoln Center, staged by Harold Clurman, would be a belated response to the Holocaust called *Incident at Vichy*. In Lincoln Center's second season, Kazan attempted his first classic, the Jacobean-era Middleton–Rowley tragedy *The Changeling*. It was such a resounding failure that he soon resigned from the company and devoted himself entirely to directing movies.

The rivalry between Strasberg and Kazan during the early days of Lincoln Center led to the long-awaited formation of the Actors Studio Company, partly because Strasberg was miffed over being excluded, both as teacher and director, from the Kazan initiative. But the Actors Studio Company was a short-lived undertaking, proving only what was already known, that Strasberg had the telephone numbers of a lot of movie stars. The Kazan company was dedicated, at least in principle, to training a permanent resident group of actors to perform in modern and classical plays. The Strasberg company was largely a group of Hollywood tourists slumming on Broadway. Paul Newman and Joanne Woodward were encouraged to perform in a trifle called *Baby Want a Kiss*. Franchot Tone was persuaded to star in a version of O'Neill's *Strange Interlude*. And Kim Stanley, Geraldine Page, and Kevin McCarthy were invited to perform in Strasberg's production of Chekhov's *Three Sisters* which, though it received some good notices in New York, was hooted off the stage during its London tour, despite the replacement of McCarthy by George C. Scott. A venture that for years had promised to prove the practical artistry of Strasberg's theories, to show that he was not just a master teacher but a world-class director, ended after its first season in anger and acrimony, with Strasberg (in London) repudiating his own company, and George C. Scott threatening to punch him in the nose.

This was the decade when Stephen Sondheim, writing not just lyrics now but also the scores for his works, was beginning to revolutionize the musical form with stories of failed relationships (*Company*), and serial murder (*Sweeney Todd*) and show business quarrels (*Follies*) and unfeeling artists (*Sunday in the Park with George*). His musical about political assassinations (*Assassins*) reflected on a decade when first Jack Kennedy, then Martin Luther King, then Bobby Kennedy had been assassinated, and King's Civil Rights movement was morphing into Malcolm X's Black Power. This was a decade that saw the outbreak of a new war, declared after a fictitious incident in the Tonkin Gulf (not the first, or the last, concocted occasion for an unnecessary conflict). It was to revolutionize American college campuses and forever change the way young people regarded their government.

This was also the decade that produced the psychedelic imaginings of a brilliant new playwright, Sam Shepard, with such works as *La Turista* (1967) and *The Tooth of Crime* (1972), a piece about a pair of warring rock stars. These plays by a handsome, gap-toothed, corn-fed kid from Illinois were often drug-induced, rock-influenced fantasies that displayed more energy than sense, that is, until Shepard went to London in 1972 to sit at the feet of Harold Pinter and experienced an artistic conversion. Thenceforth, his vision, without losing any of its metaphysical thrust, would be realized within domestic environments, as he investigated the secrets of the American family. These included his best works: *Buried Child* (1978), *Curse of the Starving Class* (1978), *True West* (1980), and *A Fool for Love* (1983). After going to Hollywood as an actor, Shepard would experience a third evolution, into a strong antiwar writer, with *States of Shock* in 1991, a play about the first Iraq conflict, and *The God of Hell* in 2004, about the second. But *Buried Child* would be the *locus classicus* of Shepard's career, with its hidden ("conscience of the king") metaphor about how the sins of a country are inevitably exhumed to haunt the national soul.

Antiwar Protest

In 1966, an important theatrical event occurred: the producer Joseph Papp began supplementing his summer seasons of Shakespeare in the Park with winter seasons of new plays in a renovated building called The New York Public Theatre, formerly the Astor Place Library. Papp initiated his first winter season with a production of *Hair*, a rock musical with an impudent antiwar stance. Both Galt McDermott's music and James Rado and Gerome Ragni's book for *Hair*, another antiwar piece, would have a strong influence on future musicals, especially after Tom O'Horgan directed it on Broadway. This event was followed by a cheeky interpretation of *Hamlet* starring Martin Sheen doing Shakespeare soliloquies with a Latino accent. It was at the Public, too, that the antiwar veteran David Rabe emerged as Papp's first resident playwright with such surgical attacks on the Vietnam conflict as *Pavel Hummel* and *Sticks and Bones*. And it was to the Public that Papp began attracting a number of young dramatists, writing what he called "hunchback plays," designed to provoke and upset their audiences. (In the next decade, ironically, Papp would also develop one of the most successful musicals in Broadway history—Michael Bennett's *A Chorus Line*—after a downtown workshop at the Public.)

In the same period, an experimental break-off from the Living Theatre called the Open Theatre, led by Living Theatre alumnus Joseph Chaikin, was also producing antiwar musicals such as *Viet Rock*, not to mention such straight plays as Jean-Claude van Itallie's powerful assault on motel culture called *American Hurrah!* And it was in the 1960s that the resident theater movement, already represented by the Guthrie Theatre in Minneapolis and the Arena in Washington, DC, exploded with a whole new group of decentralized, not-for-profit institutions, thus realizing Hallie Flanagan's vision of an American theater that was affordable, diverse, and decentralized. Not just American playwriting but also American institutional theater was coming of age.

Politics in the 1970s was dominated by black power protest, campus unrest, and radical activists agitating against an unjust war that was costing thousands of American and Vietnamese lives every day. Radicals had staged the Days of Rage in 1969, protesting the arrest of the Chicago Seven. Also in the late 1960s, the Living Theatre had been closed down by the IRS for failure to pay its taxes. And when Beck and Malina broke Federal locks in order to stage an unauthorized showing of *The Brig* in 1963, they were arrested and brought into court. In the Marx Brothers-style trial that followed, Judith Malina, donning her "Portia" costume, put her husband on the stand to ask him about her menstrual cycles. Worse, she so hectored a friendly judge that he found them both guilty, not of defying the IRS but of insulting the bench (i.e., contempt of court). After serving a few weeks in prison, Beck and Malina went into exile with their company in Europe, where they developed a rigorous physical style (best displayed in *Frankenstein*) unfortunately accompanied by a rigorous self-righteousness, staging sit-ins in some of the very European theaters that had invited them to perform there.

Coming to Yale as a result of my invitation, the Living Theatre ended its European exile in 1968, displaying both choreographic exactitude and defiant anarchism. As a result of this visit, the nature of the off-off-Broadway movement underwent a radical change which undermined its formerly pacifist nature. In the broader society, protest was growing violent as a wing of the Students for a Democratic Society morphed into the bomb-throwing Weather Underground, and the National Guard opened fire on students demonstrating against the war at Kent State University.

Revolution and theater in the streets were pursuing parallel paths. Then came Watergate and hearings that were to become a form of theater themselves, followed by a host of satirical revues (including *Watergate Classics* at Yale) preceding the resignation of Nixon, and finally by the conclusion of the Vietnam War. Upon succeeding Nixon as president in 1974, Gerald Ford announced that "our long national nightmare is over." What he substituted, with the help of a few sleeping pills from his successor Jimmy Carter, was a long national nap.

The 1970s also saw the emergence of another writer from Illinois, David Mamet, who, in his subtle way, was delivering a much deeper, much more subversive, much more elemental attack on the prevailing political system than the SDS or the

Weathermen with their histrionic revolutionary gestures. As the Weathermen were blowing up banks and police stations (or blowing themselves up in a house on New York's West Eleventh Street), Mamet was setting time bombs under the social order. In plays such as *American Buffalo* (1975), *Glengarry Glen Ross* (1984), and *Speed the Plow* (1988), Mamet was invidiously questioning the corporate capitalist system itself, cheerfully exposing its passionate devotion to greed and acquisition, whether in real estate or the film industry.

At the same time, having settled for a while in the university town of Cambridge, MA, he began documenting the utter absurdity and irrelevance of political correctness in the academy in such works as *Oleanna* (1992).

Oddly enough, Mamet has since become an arch-conservative. But the wry, mordant, indirect tone of Mamet's earlier work, himself a native of Chicago, was also reflected in the improvisations of Paul Sills' Second City Chicago company and in the spinoff cabaret acts of two young actors from that group, Mike Nichols and Elaine May.

As for the nation's mainstream dramatists, they had temporarily run out of steam. With the *New York Times* monopolizing taste, we were again being told that London imports were superior to our national products, except for that "native American art form," the Broadway musical.

Meanwhile, the *Times*' disrespect for the theater's elder statesmen was having a malign effect on the reputations of Miller, Williams, Albee, and Inge. Inge had committed suicide in 1973 after critics (myself regrettably included) had taken a closer look at his more celebrated work and rejected his more uncontrolled later offerings. Williams kept producing plays annually until his death in 1983 but few people came to see them. Miller created only two plays in the 1970s—*The Creation of the World and Other Business* (1972) and *The Archbishop's Ceiling* (1977)—neither of them particularly interesting or commercially successful.

Only Edward Albee managed to survive his bad notices and continue to write, turning out five plays in the course of the decade. But although one of them won a Pulitzer, he was also to suffer from critical handicaps for a while, only to be rehabilitated in 1994 with *Three Tall Women*, which won him another Pulitzer Prize. Theatrical taste at this time was being arbitrated by a very strong-minded and influential critic, Frank Rich of the *New York Times*, the man most responsible for the plethora of Broadway musicals and English imports. This led, after my *New Republic* criticism (in an article called "An Embarrassment of Riches") of the overweight influence he and his wife were exerting on the New York stage, to a fierce debate between us on the subject of critical power. (We have since become friends.)

In an interesting footnote, Joseph Papp took over the ailing Lincoln Center complex in the 1970s, commissioning the Rumanian director Andrei Serban, whose *Fragments of a Trilogy* had made such a strong impression at La Mama, to evolve a program of familiar classics reinvigorated by daring interpretations. After producing a stunning *Cherry Orchard*, featuring Irene Worth and Meryl Streep, and a powerful *Agamemnon* with John Cazale, Papp grew tired of draining his Broadway profits from *A Chorus Line* in order to entertain audiences he despised, and dropped the Lincoln Center initiative with no notice. It foundered until being taken over by his former partner, Bernard Gersten, and Andre Bishop, the former head of Playwrights Horizon, who turned the British writer Tom Stoppard into their resident playwright, and started competing with Broadway.

Race

The 1980s, which began with the resolution of the Iran hostage crisis, was a decade trademarked by the smiling visage and sonorous tones of Ronald Reagan, a president sometimes unable to distinguish his real life from his movie roles. This was the decade when the Cold War came to an end, largely as a result of Mikhail Gorbachev's efforts to humanize the Soviet Union and Boris Yeltsin's efforts to dissolve it. But aside from this important historical development, American foreign policy led to nothing more momentous than the invasion of Grenada, an action that made the world safe for duty-free shopping, as well as the Iran-Contra scandal, a scandal that made Fox News safe for Oliver North. The event was neither much noted by American drama, nor for that matter by the American public.

Instead, with Vietnam only a memory, the nation was once again beginning to explore domestic issues. Examining their own cultures were African-Americans primarily, but also a host of other American ethnic groups, including Latinos, Asians, and Jews, seeking the appropriate theatrical idioms, language, scenarios, and social postures for the purpose.

Race-based drama, with a history that started in the nineteenth century with Dion Boucicault's *The Octoroon* and George L. Aiken's dramatization of Harriet Beecher Stowe's *Uncle Tom's Cabin*, had effectively resumed in the 1960s with Leroi Jones's *Dutchman* (1964) and James Baldwin's *Blues for Mister Charlie* (1964), though surely the groundbreaking play in this genre was Lorraine Hansberry's *A Raisin in the Sun* (1959). August Wilson was now making race a major issue of the American theater. With his essentially realistic ten-play cycle, tracing the evolution of black consciousness and American racism throughout the twentieth century, Wilson had developed the largest vision of African-American writers, but the movement also included some powerful women playwrights, including Suzan-Lori Parks, Anna Deavere Smith, Ntozake Shange, and Adrienne Kennedy, who were working in freer forms.

In the 1960s, Papp, an early partisan of nontraditional casting who brought mobile units into ghetto neighborhoods, had featured African-American writers such as Ron Milner (*What the Wine Sellers Buy*) and George C. Wolfe (*Spunk, The Colored Museum*), injecting what had hitherto been a marginal fringe expression into the mainstream. (Wolfe was to become Papp's successor following the producer's death in 1991.) At the same time, Robert Macbeth's New Lafayette Theatre (staging plays such as Ed Bullins' *The Electronic Nigger*) and the Douglas Turner Ward and Robert Hooks' Negro Ensemble Theatre (producing Lonnie Elder's *Ceremonies in Dark Old Men* and Charles Fuller's *A Soldier's Play*) were making major contributions to African-American drama as well.

With Wilson, however, plays that might have been previously confined to off- or off-off-Broadway stages were now being cycled through the resident theater movement, first premiering at Yale under Lloyd Richards before circulating their way to Broadway.

Wilson had developed a very exclusionary racial perspective, once asserting for example that African-American actors should only appear in plays by African-American playwrights.

I debated this issue with him in 1997 at Town Hall, apprehensive that such an idea could rob the theater, not to say, the movies, of some extraordinary performances. (I had earlier run into a similar kind of debate in reverse with Samuel Beckett, who protested because the ART had cast two African-Americans in *Endgame*.)

But despite these odd self-segregating gestures, Wilson was becoming one of the giants of the American stage, winning a number of Tonys and Pulitzers and being placed on the same plateau as O'Neill, Williams, and Miller.

The 1980s were also a time for the emergence or reemergence of writers such as Jules Feiffer (*Grown Ups* 1981), Christopher Durang (*Sister Mary Ignatius Explains It All for You*, 1981, *The Marriage of Bette and Boo*, 1985), Wendy Wasserstein (*Isn't It Romantic*, 1983, *The Heidi Chronicles*, 1988), Wallace Shawn

(*Marie and Bruce*, 1978, and *Aunt Dan and Lemon*, 1985), and John Guare (*Lydie Breeze*, 1982, and *Six Degrees of Separation*, 1990), all with strong satirical strains, while Marsha Norman (with *'night Mother*, 1983) was turning the kitchen drama into a form of psychological tragedy.

At the same that serious drama was exploring race and ethnicity, the American musical was exploring itself with dozens of revivals, or inflating big empty Andrew Lloyd-Webber balloons like *Cats* and *Phantom of the Opera*, where the spectacle of flying saucers and falling chandeliers distracted you from the weakness of the music or the inanity of the plot. Without a major foreign war, the theater had turned inward, toward domestic issues, finding its expression in tribal affirmations, identity politics, or empty spectacle.

Sexuality

Part social protest, part personal statement, the race-based study of the self was a form of theatrical expression that has continued to the present day, meanwhile extending into an affirmation of gay pride and feminism. The 1990s was a decade dominated by plays by or about gays and women, the most impressive example of these being Tony Kushner's epic *Angels in America* in two parts (*Millennium Approaches* and *Perestroika*), which debuted on Broadway in 1993 after a number of workshops and productions elsewhere.

Angels in America was hardly the first gay protest play. Mart Crowley's *The Boys in the Band* (1970) was a strong introduction to the feline wit of the homosexual community, David Henry Hwang's *M. Butterfly* combined gay and Asian themes in 1988, and Larry Kramer and Terrence McNally had been writing gay protest plays for years. (Indeed, McNally's brave *Corpus Christi* in 1998, about a homosexual Jesus with gay disciples, brought death threats to the leaders of the Manhattan Theatre Club and almost closed the theater down.) There was, besides, a growing literature surrounding AIDS and the country's failure, either through inefficiency or indifference, to discover a cure.

Indeed, gay activist drama was becoming such a commonplace that gay writers like Christopher Durang (*Betty's Summer Vacation*) and Paul Rudnick (*The Most Fabulous Story Ever Told*) felt perfectly comfortable about satirizing it. But the wonderfully intelligent Kushner was the first to assimilate the issue of discrimination against gays into a larger political context, particularly in his handling of the homosexual yet homophobic Roy Cohn. To this heady brew, he added a metaphysical dimension that gave the play intelligence, depth, breadth, style, and amplitude.

Also in the 1990s, a number of gifted women, both gay and straight, were looking at social issues with a discriminating subtlety unusual on our stage, while (in the case of Paula Vogel teaching at Brown, and Marsha Norman at the Juilliard School) passing the torch to others through the training process.

Among the feminist playwrights, Vogel (who took over the playwriting program at Yale) has emerged as among the most sophisticated and textured of the women writers, largely because she never strictly toed the feminist party line. In an AIDS play like *The Baltimore Waltz* (1992) but particularly in *Hot n' Throbbing* (1994) and *How I Learned to Drive* (1997), Vogel dealt with red-button topics such as female pornography and sexual abuse in a manner that kept them fresh and surprising.

As for musicals, Jonathan Larsen's *Rent* (1996), with its strong gay themes, became the longest-running piece of the time (William Finn's *Falsetto* trilogy, produced in the 1980s being a forerunner). *Rent* was a product of the enterprising New York Theatre Workshop which, along with Elizabeth LeCompte's Wooster Group and of course the Public

Theatre, was producing much of the interesting theater material in New York, then as now.

As a result of the uproar surrounding NEA grants to Robert Mapplethorpe and Andres Serrano (a replay of HUAC's reaction to the Federal Theatre), the National Endowment had been cut back drastically in its funding and had lost its nerve. This, along with cuts in foundation and corporate support, was making the American nonprofit theater timid and hesitant, both toward the kinds of plays being considered and the way they could be done. For example, the collective impulse that found its expression in resident acting companies was dissolving now into an individualist aesthetic that depended on stars from a variety of media. Audiences were once again going to shows with pick-up casts rather than those of resident companies, Broadway style, with no sense that a theater was an organism capable of growth as well.

In short, the resident theater movement, once the proud flagship of experimental American theater, was growing more and more indistinguishable from Broadway, in the quality of its fare, its relationship to New York producers, the structure of its seasons, and the aging of its audiences.

Beyond the Millennium

The American Century came to an abrupt end on September 11, 2001, when two airplanes, hijacked by Muslim extremists, crashed into the twin towers of the World Trade Center. American territory had been attacked before, but never, since the Revolutionary War, the American mainland. The myth of an impregnable exceptionalist state imparting higher values, more sophisticated politics, and more expensive commodities to a benighted world was coming to an end.

The Bush response to 9/11 was to invade Afghanistan in a vain quest for Osama Bin Laden, and soon after, under the pretext of neutralizing the use of weapons of mass destruction by Saddam Hussein, to invade Iraq. When the WMDs failed to materialize, the administration had to content itself with hanging Saddam and inventing other motives for the war—making the Mid-East safe from autocracy, Iraq safe from Al-Qaeda, and America safe from terror, while pursuing an endlessly escalating war with an indefinable goal.

In the meantime, our country was defending itself against terror through terrorist tactics, practicing torture at Abu Ghraib and elsewhere, incarcerating hundreds of Muslims without trial in Guantanamo, eavesdropping without warrant on its own citizens, and enriching a tiny corporate majority at the expense of an increasingly disenfranchised middle class, a process that has now led to economic disorder.

Meanwhile, a large number of the world's nations, even those under the protection of the United States, were beginning to implode, first in Europe, then in Africa. Kosovo, Darfur, Ethiopia, Uganda, Zimbabwe, Sudan, these names were becoming synonymous with genocide; a new Cold War appeared to be starting with Russia; China was preparing to dominate the upcoming century. And at home, the economy was beginning to tank, aided by such natural disasters as Hurricane Katrina and by such human disasters as the collapse of the mortgage market. The detritus left behind by the American Century was being scattered all over the land.

As for the stage, it was, as usual, slow in following these developments (the favored medium now was the blogosphere). As in film, where the few movies made about Iraq—notably *In the Valley of Elah*, *Rendition*, and *Stop-Loss*—were box office failures. American theater was proving unable to attract audiences to plays dramatizing the impact of the war on the American character and economy, that is, when the theater bothered with this subject at all. The Pulitzer Prize for Drama in 2008, for example, went to Tracy Letts'

August: Osage County, an admittedly strong drama about the breakdown of a family but one that gave no indication of a world elsewhere, performed on a set that could have been used in any number of previous domestic dramas, whether *A Long Day's Journey*, *Death of a Salesman*, or *Buried Child*. With the continuous exposure of malfeasance and deception in the government, and burgeoning sentiment against the war, radical resistance would begin building again in the theater after the 2004 election of George W. Bush, though the absence of a draft continued to prevent antiwar sentiment from reaching anti-Vietnam proportions. Still, the theater managed to produce *Omnium Gatherum*, an imaginative treatment of 9/11 by Theresa Rebeck and Alexandra Gersten-Vassilaros, and Sam Shepard's penetrating metaphor about America's torture practices, *The God of Hell*. Tony Kushner's prescient *Homebody/Kabul*, written about Afghanistan right before 9/11, was another example of our theater's engagement with America's troubled foreign policy. But his musical *Caroline or Change* (2002), about the relations between a black maid and a Jewish family in the American South, seemed more typical of the smaller-scale personal and domestic interests of our time.

Once again, as America faced the 2008 election, Broadway's face was turned away from the outside world, grinding out safe musical works and reviving old commercial favorites, as our nation lumbered nervously along, uncertain how to redefine its shattered identity or redeem its lost honor.

But the millennium witnessed the emergence of a number of major playwrights (Stephen Adly Guirgis, Tracy Letts, Charles L. Mee, Jr., Doug Wright, Adam Rapp, Richard Nelson, Sarah Ruhl, Lynn Nottage, Richard Nelson, Rebecca Gilman, and Moises Kaufman among them), who are still going strong, on par with O'Neill in their seriousness of purpose if not in the magnitude of their achievement. All of them are poised to do what the stage has done so well throughout this century, look unblinkingly into the eye of a Gorgon without turning to stone. The recent history of our country has exposed deep flaws in the American character and the American political system, both its foreign policy and domestic behavior. The theater is uniquely positioned to describe these fissures. It cannot claim to cure them—that is not a faculty of the highest art—but rather to understand them better through appropriate plots, characters, and metaphors. For only through understanding them will the means be found to bear our national afflictions and find the road to change. And in how many places besides the theater can fading ideals be reconstituted and refreshed, and political and cultural scars be burned and purged away? (2008).

2

Arab Spring Forward, Fall Back

The chaos we are witnessing these days in the Middle East reflects not only a failure of American policy but also a pitiful lack of American self-knowledge. Despite a lack of dynamic government in Washington, we have been trying to convince the Arab world that every Middle Eastern nation would be better off practicing our native brand of constitutional democracy. One might hope for a little more modesty about one's own political achievements, considering that the United States has become as paralyzed and disordered as any democracy in Europe or South America. But instead of trying to perfect, or at least improve, ourselves, we prefer to urge our dysfunctional system on the rest of the world.

This pridefulness partly explains our indecision over the recent protests in Egypt. The United States has played a greater or lesser part in most of the convulsions of the Arab Spring, that herculean effort by the people of Egypt, Libya, Tunisia, Yemen, Morocco, the Sudan, Syria, and other Arab nations to overhaul their failing governments. In most cases, demonstrators were trying to import democratic rule into countries led for years by strong men (sultans, generals, kings, sheikhs, and dictators), and there is no doubt that we have done a lot to cheer them on. First, the Bush regime toppled

Saddam Hussein on the pretext that Iraq had weapons of mass destruction. Next we brought down the Taliban in Afghanistan, settling for a corrupt secular administration in place of a repressive religious order. Then Libya's Khadaffi fell, to be replaced by a "representative" form of government not even competent enough to prevent terrorist acts against the US embassy. Then President Assad of Syria was almost toppled by a coalition that included Al-Qaeda-influenced Sunni factions—until the Shiite Hezbollah stepped in and reversed the tide. Then after Egypt's Hosni Mubarak's overthrow led to a democratically elected government headed by Mohamed Morsi and the Muslim Brotherhood, that was also toppled following protests by secular factions, resulting in a coup by the Egyptian army.

In a few cases, it seemed as if the people were not so much replacing an Arab political leader as substituting a competing religious ideology. Sunnis and Shiites, the largest of the Muslim factions, are not just political opponents within one country, like the North and the South in the American Civil War, or the Communists and Fascists in 1930s' Spain. They are religious adversaries spread throughout the Middle East, locked in a struggle to overcome each other in a way that sometimes made the civil wars of the past look like minor scuffles. Each "awakening" in the Arab Spring may have started as a political conflict between liberal and conservative factions, or between left-wing and right-wing ideologies. But our eyes soon opened on bombings and shootings between opposing religious factions, not to mention by the military bloc that recently killed fifty unarmed people in Egypt.

And here lies the problem for American policy. The democratic elections we are encouraging in the Middle East often end up in victory either for Islamic factions fundamentally hostile to the American presence or for a corrupt secular government eager for our financial support, but not our military help (*vide* Iraq and Afghanistan). Our naïve belief that all the peoples in the Arab world prefer a system of rule that separates Church from State has inevitably led us to bet on the wrong horses in the Middle East.

After our experience with Maliki in Iraq, who is cuddling up to Iran, and with Karzai in Afghanistan, who has been using his office to loot the state treasury, it should have been obvious that such changes rarely advance US interests in the area. Take Morsi as an obvious example, a man legitimately elected, who immediately tried to impose the Muslim Brotherhood on the rest of Egypt.

In a recent column in the *New York Times*, David Brooks suggested that state control by the Egyptian army was preferable to the democratically elected rule of the Muslim Brotherhood. Embarrassing as it is for a democratic people to admit this, our own interests in Egypt—ideally served by a duly-elected secular majority—are often just as endangered by a democracy of religious extremists as by autocratic one-man rule. At least, the autocrats (Iran's Ayatollah Khomenei being a notable exception) are rarely tyrants—and never extremists, encouraging people to blow themselves up in crowded marketplaces.

In a recent article in *Newsweek*, my step-son Peter Beinart eloquently argued that "The answer to Morsi's perversion of Egyptian democracy should have been more democracy," and admonished David Brooks for saying that Islamists have "absolutist, apocalyptic mind-sets." "Islam," he writes, "comes in different, and sometimes mutually hostile, varieties." That is certainly true, but isn't that mutual hostility responsible for most of the troubles in the area? In Egypt, it certainly looks as though a freely elected theocracy, toppled by the coup of the generals, was leading the people into civil war. We are in a dilemma. Strong man rule, as proposed recently by King Abdullah of Saudi Arabia, is undoubtedly repressive. But it might be more effective than democracy in dealing with the kind of explosive terror we often see these days in Iraq, Afghanistan, Lebanon, and Libya.

Actually, it may be that authoritarian leadership represents the natural order of things in the Middle East. It has certainly been a Middle East practice ever since the Ottoman Empire started in the fifteenth century, and it has had the comforting advantage of exercising secular control over religious fanaticism. During the Ottoman Empire and after, the Muslim faith was freely practiced, along with Christianity and Judaism, but religion was never allowed a role in government.

Am I arguing that we should remain silent while repressive regimes are being installed throughout the Middle East? No, just that we should stop pressing our influence in an area where nobody seems to want our advice. And that, it seems, is what the Obama administration has also concluded, the evidence being its withdrawal of troops from Iraq and Afghanistan, and now its quietist attitude toward the Egyptian crisis (what is being called "assessing the situation"). For all our financial leverage, the United States has no lasting influence on politics in the Middle East. And we really have no way to prevent political change except through more ill-fated intervention.

Yes, there may be human rights violations under any kind of rule in the Middle East. But while human rights groups should pursue those violations relentlessly, and while our own government should use whatever means necessary to protest any curbs on free speech, our best course is to cease any activity in the area, except to help broker a peace between Israel and Palestine.

Overzealous interventionists like Senator McCain would do well to realize that imposing our will on other countries has done nothing but exacerbate Middle Eastern political troubles, when we are having enough difficulty solving our own. If this sounds like isolationism, well, so be it. Just consider what, aside from the loss of countless American lives, our interventionism has accomplished in Vietnam, in the Bay of Pigs, in Grenada, Haiti, Iran, Somalia, Iraq, Afghanistan, and everywhere else in the Middle East (2013).

3

Theater and the University: Marriage or Misalliance

I would like to discuss the wedding between the professional theater and the university—a marriage that is now about fifty years old. Has this union been a happy and productive one? Or a relationship more likely to lead to marital squabbling and divorce proceedings than to loving toasts at golden anniversary celebrations?

Speaking of golden anniversaries, I can exploit my venerability as an ancient mariner, since I was in on this twentieth century theatrical union almost from the very beginning. I had borrowed the idea to start a professional repertory theater closely connected to the Yale Drama School from an entity known as the Stanford Repertory Theater, started in the mid-1960s by Robert Loper, after he had invited two professional actors from New York to teach his drama students and join them in productions.

This struck me as a very intriguing concept. Remembering that most of the great theaters were attached to training programs—the Comedie Francaise, the old Vic, the Moscow Art Theater, the Berliner Ensemble among them—I hoped to import and extend the Stanford idea to the Yale School of Drama.

I thought a professional theater would be necessary at Yale as a model for students in training, whether actors, playwrights, directors, designers, technicians, administrators, or dramaturgs. It had the potential to provide a flow of gifted teachers, as well as being a destination for theater people after graduation, even a laboratory in which they could work preceding graduation. In short, our students were being trained for the newly created American resident theater movement, and specifically as permanent company members, the reasoning being that every theater needed new ideas and fresh young blood to keep it alive.

I wasn't alone in this idea. By coincidence, a brilliant young theater artist named William Ball, with whom I used to act in the 1950s at Wellesley's Theatre on the Green, and with whom I shared a Fulbright year in England, was starting a unit he called the American Conservatory Theater with very similar artistic and training goals in virtually the same time period. After Ball's death, and under his successor, Carey Perloff, it remains one of the shiny buttons of the movement.

I persuaded Yale to accept the Rep by comparing it to the relationship between the Medical School and the Yale New Haven Hospital in that, like doctors who worked side by side with their medical students and residents examining patients and doing basic research, theater students and theater professionals could together generate a similar combination of talent, ideas, and cures. Was this an easy marriage? No, but I think it managed to work despite some Old Blue grumbling, radical disruptions, the Black Panther May Day, opposition to the "elitist" master-apprentice system, and other inevitable obstacles; and at Yale, it is continuing to work under a Dean of genuine integrity and vision, James Bundy.

A number of emerging professional theaters were soon to follow this model, either by developing schools or by starting programs tightly or loosely connected with nearby universities—The Guthrie and the University of Minnesota, UCLA and the Geffen Theater, Brown and the Trinity Rep, Harvard and the ART, Princeton and the McCarter Theater, Boston University and the Huntington, Suffolk University and the Modern Theatre, and so forth.

It is no secret that the ideal of the permanent resident company, so central to any training program, and to the theater's relationship with the university, has been seriously eroded by fiscal and board constraints, partly due to the economy, partly to the fickleness of private foundations, partly to red state congressional hostility toward the NEA. The resident theater movement had originally been formed as an alternative to the profit-making theater, not as an extension of it. Its guiding principle was hardly to be a farm team for the major leagues on a quest after enhancement money, but a generator of new techniques, new plays, new approaches to the classics in order to advance the art of the theater. In its ideal form, it was to be devoted to the establishment and maintenance of an artistic collective for the purpose of shared work and common artistic growth—in contrast to the greedy Wall Street example of individual self-aggrandizement.

The company ideal appealed to many professional actors—in our first year we managed to attract such gifted and often emerging artists as Stacy Keach, Linda Lavin, Ron Leibman, Jeremy Geidt, Kathleen Widdoes, Eugene Troobnick, Anthony Holland, Alvin Epstein, John Bottoms, Remo Airaldi, Estelle Parsons, Cherry Jones, John Douglas Thompson, Irene Worth, and Kenneth Haigh—even Stella Adler, our principal acting teacher, spent ten minutes considering a return to the stage as Madame Arkadina in a production of *The Seagull.*

As for audiences, they were a union of engaged participants paying ticket prices affordable to every income group, rather than a coterie of expense account tourists, pouring out the equivalent of a three-day vacation in Barbados for a single Broadway show. And one never had to make the work "accessible" through awkward, condescending popularizing. If it was immediate and engaged, they got it.

The country never fully embraced this concept because it has not yet fully grown up as a culture. And America's continuing adolescence in regard to support for the arts helps explain why the so-called not-for-profit theater is now sometimes serving less as an alternative to the Broadway system than as a tryout house for commercial interests. I'm certainly not suggesting that these two systems shouldn't have relations with each other, or even intermarry at times. Rather, I am criticizing a process in which commercial interest is aroused before the opening of a not-for-profit production and thereby has a hand in raising the baby.

And now it is time for confession. I may have been the one who unconsciously initiated this process after Rocco Landesman, a former student and teacher at the ART, brought me a play called *Big River* by another former student, William Hauptmann, and then handed me a score for it he had wangled out of Roger Miller. Aside from a small percentage of the gross, we never profited much from the Broadway transfer he made, but this was precisely the kind of thing I had been criticizing, and continue to deplore. Rocco remains one of my greatest friends and, at the same time, my greatest source of personal embarrassment.

Fiscal pressure explains this kind of commercial outreach, but doesn't excuse it. For if the earlier relationship between the not-for-profit theater and the university may have sometimes been a scene of marital strife, the extension of nonprofits into the commercial theater is, in my opinion, a serious misalliance, which may ultimately lead to a divorce between the professional theater and its host. Try to imagine how an institution of higher learning would react to a chemistry department whose professors develop new pharmaceuticals in return for enhancement money from Pfizer. (Well, come to think of it, that is precisely what is happening in some chemistry departments today! And, as a matter of fact, some university presidents are welcoming the commercialization of their theaters as well.)

Clearly, the arm of corporate interest is now extending into almost every area of nonprofit endeavor. It is difficult to adhere to an ideal when virtually the whole culture is in an amorous corporate embrace. But any alternative to that ideal will ultimately lead to divorce—not just between our country and its culture, but between our country and its soul (2013).

4

How to Love Your Country

One of the more depressing political attacks in recent history was launched by the patriologue former mayor of New York, Rudolph Giuliani, against President Obama. With strong implications of racism, Giuliani claimed that Obama did not love his country and might have "socialist" or "anti-colonial" leanings because of his mixed parentage and overseas birth. An even more pressing reason? Obama had suggested that we might be wrong in our blanket condemnation of the whole Muslim world as "terrorists." Reminding us that Christians had also terrorized many Muslims during the Crusades, Obama took the position that guilt, like revenge, was a dish that was best served cold.

I happen to believe with Giuliani that, despite the mess we created in the Muslim world under President George W. Bush, terrorist groups such as Isis and Boko Haram have created a new level of brutal behavior in Arab countries that more centrist Islamists are not doing enough to confront and defeat. But disagreement, in an advanced democracy such as our own, is not the same as blanket dismissal. To charge Obama with a lack of patriotism simply because he doesn't think the present conduct of our country is perfect is to assume a posture that comes perilously close to exclusionism.

This attitude of people like Giuliani and many of his fellow Republicans would not be so disturbing were it not the reigning posture of a growing number of countries, not all of them Muslim, where any deviation from strict religious or political ideology is usually punished with public condemnation, excommunication, imprisonment, torture, or death. Even in such open democracies as Israel, many supporters of Netanyahu's right-wing government have grown accustomed to charging critics of his regime, most of them Jewish, with anti-Semitism or Jewish self-hatred. Repressive reaction to criticism, we should remember, has been a central feature of North Korea, Russia, and some parts of China, among others. And now, under our Republican-dominated House and Senate, anything perceived as opening our land to immigrants or exiles, or improving the lot of the unemployed, has become grounds for shutting down the government, or impeaching and suing the president. This from the Congressional welfare cheats who spend most of their terms loafing in their home states, collecting paychecks.

Giuliani, and the political forces he represents, one suspects, are really the ones who don't love America, because they are circulating the undemocratic notion that to love your country you must embrace all its faults. This was hardly the position of the founding fathers, with their commitment to liberty and justice for all. It was not the position of Abraham Lincoln who sacrificed his popularity, not to mention his own life, to put an end to our primal sin of slavery. It was not the position of Franklin Delano Roosevelt, whose New Deal created countless laws protecting the rights of the persecuted and the homeless. It was not the position of Lyndon Johnson, who helped overcome the continuing exposure of African-Americans to persecution, inequality, and contempt. And it has certainly never been the position of Barack Obama, who has devoted his presidency to securing the economy, improving immigration laws, equalizing sexual opportunity, and evolving a sensible and humane way to protect our interests overseas without excessive violence.

It is one of the great advantages of our democracy that it protects even the speech of bigots like Giuliani. Indeed, it protects any form of speech short of incitements to violence. It also protects the right of our much-maligned president to implement his policies. We'll leave it to history—and our descendants—to decide which of these behavior patterns demonstrate more love of country (2015).

5

Shakespeare's Absent Queen

Shakespeare's *Hamlet* ends with anguished concern ("How Does the Queen?") about the well-being of Gertrude, whose accidental death by a poisoned chalice may be why her son finally decides to take arms against her husband Claudius. Indeed, queens and mothers figure prominently in almost all of Shakespeare's plays, including women as potentially dangerous to their offspring as Lady Macbeth, who would even have dashed out her little baby's brains to prove her dedication.

But where is the suffering queen or even homocidal mother in *King Lear*? The play proceeds for five full acts without a single hint that Lear was ever married, or that his three children ever enjoyed the slightest touch of maternal care. And this omission is not only in the main plot. It characterizes the subplot as well, where although the Earl of Gloucester has a castle and a province, he is not provided with a countess.

These women are not only absent from the play. They don't ever seem to have existed. When Lear was dividing his kingdom you would think that Cordelia might have asked what her mother's opinion would have been of his behavior.

But the word "mother" is used only twice in the play. Once it is a reference to Lear's irrepressible grief: "Oh, how this mother swells up towards my heart, Hysterica Passio, down, thou climbing sorrow down. Thy element's below." And once when the Fool mocks Lear for giving power to his children—"ever since thou madest thy daughters thy mothers. For when thou gavest them the rod, and put'st down thy own breeches, then they for sudden joy did weep."

At least two things ought to be noted in the first passage. First, that Lear associates femininity with excessive emotion, and tempestuous conduct with female behavior. And second, that "Hysterica passio" is located "below," which is to say in the lower regions of the body. As a matter of fact, the word hysteria is actually derived from the Greco-Roman word "hystera" or uterus, and may have been originally applied to women by Hippocrates.

The thing to note about the Fool's remarks is that mothers are associated with corporal punishment ("when thou gavest them [your daughters] the rod. And put'st down thy breeches"), a role usually assigned to fathers. Having given his kingdom away, Lear is in no position to exercise power over his daughters, and the only one who treats him like a loving father is his rejected offspring, Cordelia, in the concluding scenes of the play.

One possible explanation for the absence of mothers in this play, of course, may be purely statistical. Shakespeare had already used three boys employed by the Globe to play the three sisters, and there may have been no kids left to fill the roles of Lear's Queen or Gloucester's Countess. We don't actually know how many woman-playing boys were regularly employed by Shakespeare's company. Of the 147 females out of a total of 1222 characters appearing in his 37 plays, the largest number of women he ever created (in *The Winter's Tale*) was 8, the smallest (in *The Tempest*) was 1, and the average was 3. Assuming Shakespeare at this time was confined to the average would explain why we have Goneril,

Regan, and Cordelia, but no queen. Like so many playwrights before and after him, Shakespeare may have had to make his casting decisions on the basis of actors' availability.

A more speculative, and considerably more controversial, explanation is one inspired by Stephen Greenblatt's conviction in *Will in the World* that some of the stranger things in Shakespeare works can be partially explained through his personal experience. As far as we know, Shakespeare had no particular difficulties with his mother, the former Mary Arden of Warwickshire, who gave birth to eight children, two of whom died in infancy.

But Mary was not the only mother in his life. There was also his wife, Anne Hathaway, eight years older than he was, who provided him with three children, the first—Susanna—born six months after the marriage ceremony, and the second his twins, Judith and Hamnet (who died of plague at the age of eleven). The age gap suggests an enforced marriage as a result of premarital pregnancy.

Susanna's first child was also conceived before her marriage. And Judith's marriage was full of scandal, largely because of the philandering nature of her husband, Thomas Quiney.

This is probably the reason why Shakespeare left the bulk of his estate to Susanna, a much smaller amount to Judith, and only his "second-best bed" to his wife, Anne. Might there be echoes here, first of the division in Lear's kingdom, and second, of the resentment Lear feels towards Goneril and Regan? And is it not vaguely possible that in obliterating Lear's Queen, Shakespeare may also have been trying to erase his own wife from history? (2015).

6

School for Crime

Recent events are proving the old theorem that a criminal record, or least the promise of a criminal proceeding, has become an essential requirement for holding or pursuing political office. Sexual scandal, of course, has always been a condition of political life—*vide* Francois Hollande of France, simultaneously cheating on three different women or Anthony Weiner preening his weiner on the Internet (now a movie documentary in a theater near you).

But the epidemic of corruption, theft, plagiarism, bribe-taking, bridge blocking, and just plain venality that now characterizes public life has become unprecedented since the "avaritia" of the ancient Romans, whose passion for greed and luxury set a standard that American politicians have long ago surpassed. Even the Nixon administration, with its passion for dirty tricks, looks spotless compared to our present condition. Now both Democrats and Republicans can boast of real scandals based on indictable crimes.

If you put the parties on a scale, the Republicans would no doubt have the edge. Avid to protect the ill-gotten gains of its wealthiest constituents, the party has been converting the money-laundering techniques of the 1 percent into prime political stratagems.

Some time ago, there was the case of former Virginia Republican governor, Bob McDonnell, convicted with his wife, Maureen, of taking $160,000 in bribes from a constituent in return for business favors (in return, McDonnell bribed the donor with the favors of his wife). Then, there was the case of the Republican governor of Texas, Rick Perry, who was indicted on two felony counts for illegally trying to dump his Democratic attorney general.

Four of the last seven Illinois governors, ending with Democrat Rod Blagojevich in 2011, have spent time in prison for corruption. And if we count American mayors, then jail time, either before, during, or after serving in office, seems to be almost a precondition for the job.

Typical of the syndrome is Dennis Hastert, the Illinois Republican Speaker of the House, who was accused of molesting at least four boys in their locker room or at a motel while coaching wrestling at Yorkville High School. He was recently sentenced to fifteen months in state prison.

And now we have the opposing candidates for president of the United States qualifying for office by being accused of criminal action. Hillary Clinton has been cited for conducting government business on her own official stationary, which, though it appears to be more an epistolary error than a felony, has been cited by the FBI as a potential crime. And Donald Trump is raising suspicions for refusing to release his tax returns, though every previous candidate has done so.

Rather than force all these unfortunate politicians to undergo hurtful publicity and public humiliation after taking office, there ought to be some way to short-circuit the process and make life easier for them.

Here is what I propose. Why not set up an independent school inside the prison system where people running for higher office could get higher honors in crime, combining their criminal records with their school records, and graduating with an advanced degree in felony? This would put the heavy financial burden for indicting his or her own crimes on the politician rather than the state, and permit the media to reserve even more air time for overreported "Breaking News" like the Malaysian Flight 347 and the Boeing EgyptAir crashes. It would also position the candidate for election without the distractions (and expenses) of indictments, court time, convictions, and prison time.

Courses and seminars at the School for Crime might include How to Shake Hands Without Exposing the Check (*Bribery 101*), How to Remain in Office as a Convicted Criminal (*Persistence 404*), How to Ignore All Requests for the Truth (*Muddle the Facts 505)*, How to Send Email Without Attracting Attention *(HillaryPost 202)*, How to Keep Us Guessing about the Size of Your Hands (*TrumpFingers 303)*. Wankers of the World unite! You have nothing to lose but your ankle chains! (2016).

7

Dynasties

George Washington turned down a third presidential term because he did not wish to emulate the British system of lifetime rule. In contrast to this selfless democratic gesture, we now have something resembling a system of successive family presidencies, otherwise known as dynastic rule.

The early years of the Republic saw only one example of the dynastic impulse: John Adams and his son John Quincy Adams. The twentieth and twenty-first century presidencies, however, are almost a register of family successions, starting with Franklin Delano Roosevelt.

Roosevelt outraged a number of Americans, largely in the Republican Party, by accepting (though not quite completing) a fourth term. As a result, the Supreme Court passed the 22nd Amendment limiting presidential candidates to two four-year terms. Never again did a Roosevelt occupy the White House, though the name continued to resound throughout the walls of the Senate, the House of Representatives, and various State offices.

Actually, dynastic rule in America began with the Kennedy family. Joseph P. Kennedy, Roosevelt's ambassador to Britain, had early decreed that his eldest son Joseph Jr. would be the Democratic candidate for president. But Joseph Jr. died prematurely in World War II. This left the next in line, John F. Kennedy, to fill the post, which he did reluctantly due to extreme back pain until his assassination in 1962.

With no Kennedys filling the office of vice president, the family had to wait until the death of Lyndon Johnson to put forth a presidential candidate. This proved to be Bobby Kennedy, who was likewise gunned down by an assassin. This left Teddy Kennedy, considered an almost certain nominee, until the Chappaquiddick incident dashed his presidential hopes (and probably rescued him from a third Kennedy assassination). Unhampered by the presidency, Teddy went on to become one of the most effective legislators in American history.

The Watergate scandals no doubt saved us from a Nixon dynasty, though Dick's daughter Julie and Dwight Eisenhower's son John had married and seemed to be waiting in the wings.

So the next presidential family dynasty became that of the Bushes, first George H. W. Bush, who lasted one term, and then his son George W. who lasted two. The next might be that of the Clintons, since Bill's scandal-ridden two-term could be dynastified in 2016 by the election of his wife, Hillary (and maybe his daughter Chelsea at a still later date?). This could potentially be followed by another member of the Bush dynasty, Jeb,[1] and possibly one of Jeb's children, George, Noel, and John as well.

Wouldn't we be better off with the British Parliamentary system now that we have adopted its Royal System of Succession?

Note

1. Jeb did try to run in 2016 but was overwhelmed by Donald Trump, who has a few family members of his waiting in the wings.

II

Dramatic Word Plays

1

Broken News

(A television studio, occupied by the moderator, Wolf Spritzer, two commentators, Greta Insufferable and Sean Inanity, and tonight's chief guest, John Boner)

SPRITZER

Good evening, ladies and gentlemen, and welcome to another edition of *Breaking News*. We are taking a pause from our unceasing investigation into the fate of Malaysian Flight 370 to bring you Breaking News about the revolutionary decision of the United States Congress to return to Washington after its seven-and-a-half month vacation. My guest tonight is Speaker of the House Congressman John Boner. He sits on my right.

BONER

Hi.

SPRITZER

Also on my right is the noted commentator from Twist the Facts News, Greta Insufferable . . .

GRETA

Hi.

SPRITZER

. . . and to her right is another celebrated Twist the Facts commentator, Sean Inanity. Twist the Facts host, Bill O'Really, sends regrets he couldn't be here tonight. He's in San Salvador meditating on some interesting stories to invent.

SEAN

Why are we all sitting on your right?

SPRITZER

So I can look more moderate. Now Congressman Boner, how do you explain your groundbreaking decision to bring Congress back to Washington this week after its almost year-long break. Was it because the cameras caught a Democrat Representative on the floor of the House on Tuesday making a speech to empty seats?

BONER

Whoa, there! A lot of Democrat seats were empty, too.

SPRITZER

Isn't that because you declared a seven-and-a-month Congressional holiday? Are you declaring an end to that now?

BONER

I wouldn't exaggerate the amount of time we are actually going to spend in Washington this week—just enough to block the Iran sellout and start Impeachment proceedings against Obama.

GRETA

Will there be a window during which you can invite Israeli Prime Minister Netanyahu to Washington to insult the President again?

BONER

No, we have enough abusive Republicans in Congress to save the Federal government such expenses.

SEAN

What about the Tea Party? How will you keep the kettle boiling if the Impeachment process succeeds?

BONER

Oh, we have other issues with which to occupy the Tea Party.

SPRITZER

Such as?

BONER

Such as all that atheist propaganda about global warming . . .

GRETA

Sure, where in the Bible does it say that the globe is getting hotter?

SEAN

I think the globe is getting colder.

SPRITZER

Then how do you explain the icecaps melting?

BONER

Winters are hotter in the North Pole. That's why I propose the Palestinians establish their two-state solution in Greenland.

SPRITZER

Any other pressing issues to keep Congress in Washington for a few days longer?

BONER

Outlawing abortion. Prohibiting contraception. Banning smelly armpits.

GRETA

Amen to all.

BONER

And abolishing masturbation and same-sex marriage.

SEAN

(Removing his hands from under the table)

Expressly forbidden in the Scriptures.

SPRITZER

Don't you also want to ban Welfare? That's a big issue with the Right.

BONER

Absolutely. No healthy economy can tolerate welfare cheats who get paid for doing no work at all.

SPRITZER

How would you define a "welfare cheat."

BONER

Anyone who stays home from his job while continuing to collect salary checks from the government.

SPRITZER

(Loaded silence)

BONER

Are you looking at me?

SPRITZER

The house was only in session 130 days this past year. That makes for a seven-and-a-half month paid vacation.

BONER

Even politicians need time once in a while to reflect, and to meet with their constituents.

SEAN

I'm with you all the way on that, Congressman Boner. But I wish the Republicans could have stayed in Washington a little longer to legislate some tax breaks for the one-percent. They are suffering enough as it is from a bad press and threats of regulation.

GRETA

And what about ObamaCare? Republicans can't sit passively by and watch the Democrat administration spend all that Federal money on free medicine. That's a sure path to Socialism.

SEAN

Well, Obama *is* a Socialist. He picked up that radical ideology from his African homeland.

SPRITZER

Wasn't he born in Hawaii?

SEAN

One of those foreign places.

SPRITZER

A final question, Congressman Boner.

BONER

Yes?

SPRITZER

Why don't you ever smile? You seem to be miserable even when you're happy.

BONER

I smiled once. And I have videotapes to prove it. When Bibi Netanyahu addressed Congress in March.

SPRITZER

And apart from that?

BONER

What's to smile about? The opposition Party still controls the Presidency. And we have so little time left to stop Hillary before the 2016 election.

SEAN

Well, what about her email problem? Conducting your government affairs on a private phone can be a secret way of hiding the facts.

GRETA

Bill Clinton did the reverse. He conducted his private affairs on a government phone.

SPRITZER

Different kind of affairs. And he got impeached.

(Pressing his earpiece and listening)

Wait a minute! Wait a minute! There's some Breaking News here about Malaysian Flight 370.

SEAN

What is it? What is it?

SPRITZER

(Disappointed)

They're giving up the search.

GRETA

After only two years?

SEAN

You mean we have to abandon hope for those 227 passengers and 12 crew members?

SPRITZER

The black box finally ran out of time.

SEAN

(Patting his back)

Don't worry. There'll be another plane crash before long. Maybe with more dead passengers.

SPRITZER

(Crying)

Not with the lasting interest of Malaysian Flight 370.

(They all come over to comfort him.)

GRETA

There. There.

SPRITZER

I'm alright. Thanks.

SEAN

You can count on us, Wolf. Any time you have an airline catastrophe, we'll be here for you.

SPRITZER

Thanks for those good words.

(Drying his eyes)

Well, I am afraid we've far exceeded our allotted air time with House Speaker John Boner which is why we'll now take a half hour break for a Geico commercial. Please don't feed the salamander.

GRETA

What's up after the commercial, Wolf?

SPRITZER

Some Breaking News about the crash of the Hindenburg, German Zeppelin LZ 129. Well, thanks on the part of all our viewers to Greta Insufferable, Sean Inanity, and, of course, Congressmen Boner.

ALL

Thank you, Wolf. A pleasure to be on the program. See you soon, etc.

BONER

By the way, Wolf, I have some breaking news for you.

SPRITZER

(Eagerly)

Yes?

BONER

My name's pronounced Boehner.

(Blackout)

2

Poker Face

(The living room of Buster Keaton's shabby genteel mansion in East Los Angeles. Memorabilia of his silent film days strewn about this unusually sloppy room. Stills of Buster in his various film triumphs, including The Navigator, The General, and Limelight with Charlie Chaplin. At rise, Buster, now over seventy, is alone sitting at a poker table, drinking a beer, examining his hand. He then rises to examine, one by one, the other hands on the table.)

BUSTER

Don't raise with two pair, dummy. Wait for the full house.

(The next hand)

Draw for the flush.

(And the next)

Fold. You never know when to fold. When will you guys learn how to play five card stud?

(A bell rings. And rings. Buster looks up, puzzled, then calls:)

BUSTER

Lionel! Lionel!

(No answer)

LIONEL!!.

(Pause, as he tries to remember)

Ah, it's Sunday, goddammit.

(Buster leaves the stage. The sound of a door opening. He then enters with a man in his early forties, wearing a baseball cap)

BUSTER

Sorry.

(Very English)

It's my man's day off. What did you say your name was?

ALAN

Schneider. Alan Schneider.

BUSTER

Well, take a seat, why don't you.

(Buster fixes himself another beer without offering one to Alan.)

ALAN

(After a strained pause)

I'm really thrilled to meet you, Mr. Keaton. I've been a fan of yours since I was a kid.

BUSTER

That's nice. Not many people remember Buster Keaton any more.

ALAN

Everybody remembers Buster Keaton. You were the funniest man in silents.

BUSTER

(Looking at the poker hands)

You must be thinking about the tramp. Me they called the saddest man in silents.

(Another pause)

ALAN

(Looking at the table)

You're in the middle of a poker game?

BUSTER

I've been in the middle of this poker game since 1927.

ALAN

(Looking around)

Where are the other players?

BUSTER

Dead.

ALAN

Dead?

BUSTER

This is Irving Thalberg's hand. This is Nicholas Schenk's. And this one here belongs to Eric Campbell. He was the heavy at Essenay. The ballet dancer's company.

ALAN

The ballet dancer?

BUSTER

You know. Chaplin. The tramp.

ALAN

(Gravely)

Oh.

BUSTER

They're all dead.

(Pause)

Excepting me. The real sucker of the group is Thalberg. Always raises on two pair, the dummy. Owes me almost two million.

(Looks at Thalberg's hand again.)

ALAN

Do you always win?

BUSTER

Yeah.

ALAN

What's your secret.

BUSTER

My poker face.

ALAN

I see.

BUSTER

What's your game?

ALAN

Bridge.

BUSTER

No, I mean what's your game. What do you do for a living?

ALAN

I'm a theatre director.

BUSTER

Oh, you're that New York guy. I thought you were some sort of baseball player with that cap you're wearing.

ALAN

I always wear a baseball cap. It's my trademark. Like your poker face.

(Pause)

Did you get a chance to read the script I sent you?

BUSTER

(Going to a table to pick it up)

You mean this piece of crap? Yeah.

ALAN

You didn't like it?

BUSTER

Couldn't understand a word. What is this thing? Doesn't even have a title.

ALAN

There's the title. *Film.*

BUSTER

Yeah, I know. Film. The fancy word they give to movies nowadays. But what's the name of this so-called film?

ALAN

There's the name. *Film*. Sam likes simple titles. He once wrote a play called *Play*.

BUSTER

Who's Sam?

ALAN

Samuel Beckett. You never heard of him?

(Keaton nods No.)

I sent you a comedy of his once. *Waiting for Godot*? About those two tramps in the middle of nowhere? Bert Lahr ending up playing your part. The one you turned down.

BUSTER

Oh yeah, *Godot*

(He pronounces it "Gadotte")

I remember it now. I didn't understand a word of that one either.

ALAN

I'm sorry.

(Pause)

What about this . . . uh . . . movie? I hope you're not saying that part doesn't interest you, too.

BUSTER

Of course I'm interested. I'm no dummy. I don't turn down five thousand dollars for a three day shoot. That's the fee, right? Five thousand?

ALAN

Plus expenses.

BUSTER

Then I'm in.

ALAN

Great!

BUSTER

But the script needs fixing.

ALAN

Fixing?

BUSTER

It don't make no sense. And I wouldn't say it's a bunch of laughs either. The whole thing needs some goosing up. Maybe, my walk.

(He demonstrates)

ALAN

(Doubtful)

Sam . . . uh, I mean Mr. Beckett likes his actors to stick pretty close to his written actions.

BUSTER

(Not hearing)

One thing. You're going to have to cut out that bit with the cat. Dogs I can work with, especially chihuahuas. But not cats. Never get on stage with kids or cats.

ALAN

I'll mention it to Mr. Beckett.

BUSTER

I could do that bit where I sharpen my pencil and it gets smaller and smaller. Sure fire.

ALAN

We don't normally pad Samuel Beckett material.

BUSTER

Because you can tell your Mr. Beckett that his movie is too short. It won't last four minutes. Even if we stretched out the cat and dog business.

(Confidentially)

For a percentage of the gross I could offer some ideas about how to make it longer.

ALAN

Mr. Beckett doesn't usually accept co-authors.

KEATON

(Not hearing)

And tell him I've got to wear one of my pork pies. What do you think of this one?

(Puts it on)

ALAN

I can't imagine you doing a film without one of your hats.

BUSTER

Right. I got twelve of them, all different colors.

ALAN

I'll check it out with Mr. Beckett.

BUSTER

Check out one more thing. The lighting. I don't want any of those newfangled lighting effects. People got to see my face.

ALAN

Of course.

BUSTER

It's been my livelihood all these years.

ALAN

Of course.

BUSTER

(Relaxing a little)

We never used a script in the old days. In the Keaton studios. Just started with a character in a fix, then improvised and lollygagged until we figured out how to get him out of his trouble.

ALAN

I'm sure Mr. Beckett would be very interested in any stage business you can bring to his film.

BUSTER

Okay, it's a deal. I guess. Tell your Mr. Beckett that Buster Keaton is in.

ALAN

He'll be very happy.

(He stands up to shake Buster's hand.)

I am happy, too.

(He takes his coat.)

We start shooting in New York in six weeks.

(Holds out his hand. Keaton ignores it.)

It's been a real pleasure, Mr. Keaton.

(He exits.)

BUSTER

(Uncaps another beer, and goes back to the poker table. Hovering in turn over each player's hand)

(To Thalberg's)

You missed the full boat again, Irving.

(To Schencks's)

I wouldn't bluff on that load of crap, you dummy.

(To Campbell's)

You were right to fold.

(Triumphantly, revealing his own hand)

Four ladies.

(Buster rakes in the chips as the lights fade.)

3

Airport Hell

(A check-in desk in an airport terminal. A desk sign with the motto "Delta is ready when you are." A pleasant female attendant is busy on the phone. Eurydice Watson, carrying a large bag and a carry-on, comes up to sign in.)

EURYDICE

Miss?

ATTENDANT

I'll be with you in a moment.

(To the phone)

Well, why wouldn't she leave him? It's the fifth time he's cheated on her in a month.

(Cheerily, to Eurydice)

This won't take a moment.

EURYDICE

(Pleasant)

My plane is leaving in forty minutes. I haven't checked in. And there are long lines at security.

ATTENDANT

What plane is that?

EURYDICE

Flight 5802 to Tampa.

ATTENDANT

Oh, that flight's been cancelled. They didn't phone you?

EURYDICE

Cancelled? Why?

ATTENDANT

They never tell us. Could be weather. Could be equipment.

EURYDICE

But I have to get to Tampa today. My daughter is having a baby.

ATTENDANT

Really? Boy or girl?

EURYDICE

They think it's a baby girl.

ATTENDANT

Isn't that precious? What are they going to name her?

EURYDICE

I'm sorry. I'm in a hurry.

ATTENDANT

Of course you are. Listen, I can't help you, but I suggest you take the airport shuttle over to United at Terminal C. They have dozens of daily flights to Tampa.

EURYDICE

Thank you. You've been very kind.

ATTENDANT

(The attendant goes back to her phone call.)

So tell her to chuck the bum out of the house, and get a German shepherd.

EURYDICE

(Wanders in circles with her luggage as the attendant changes her desk card to "Fly the friendly skies of United.")

EURYDICE

I have a flight to Tampa today and the woman at Delta said . . .

ATTENDANT

(Not friendly)

Wait a minute. Please go to the back of the line.

EURYDICE

What line? I'm the only passenger here.

ATTENDANT

You jumped the queue. There are hundreds of other passengers waiting to check in, unless you are a First Class passenger, a Silver Wings Plus, or can fake a disability.

EURYDICE

I do have a disability.

(She pretends to limp.)

I sprained my ankle.

ATTENDANT

In that case, I'll take you. You're going to Tampa you say? How many bags to check?

EURYDICE

Just this one.

(The attendant takes it and puts it on the roller.)

ATTENDANT

Yes, United does have a flight to Tampa, leaving at 2:15 PM. Give me your Delta ticket.

(She rips it up.)

EURYDICE

That's great.

ATTENDANT

But it only flies on alternate Tuesdays, Thursdays, and Saturdays, except for Thanksgiving weekend, Gay Pride Week, and Shevouth, when it flies on alternate Mondays, Wednesdays, and Fridays. Unfortunately, today is Sunday, when there is no flight to Tampa. I suggest you try American in Terminal B. I believe they have a flight to Tampa this afternoon.

EURYDICE

But you just ripped up my ticket.

ATTENDANT

Not to worry. The ticket is in the computer.

EURYDICE

And you've checked my luggage.

ATTENDANT
Yes, to Tampa. Aren't you going there?

EURYDICE
On another plane.

ATTENDANT
Well, the bag would have been lost anyway.

(Proudly)

We misplace 10,000 pieces of baggage every day. Isn't that amazing? Here, fill out a claim check.

EURYDICE
Never mind. It's just a lot of baby things, and presents. I kept all my personal items in my carry-on.

ATTENDANT
Very smart. I never check bags myself.

Eurydice rolls her carry-on around in ever-widening circles, as the Attendant changes the desk card to "American Airlines: Getting there is half the fun."

EURYDICE
I was told that you might have a ticket for me on a flight to Tampa. I was on Delta Flight 5456 but the plane got cancelled.

ATTENDANT
We are flying to Tampa today, at 2:45 PM, Flight 376.

EURYDICE
Thank God.

ATTENDANT

But the plane is presently full.

EURYDICE

Oh, no.

ATTENDANT

I'd be happy to put you on a waiting list. We often get cancellations.

EURYDICE

Oh, all right.

ATTENDANT

Your best bet is to call the airline directly. They sometimes put seats aside. Here's the number. Do you have a cell phone?

EURYDICE

Yes.

(She dials it. The same attendant answers the phone.)

PHONE VOICE

Welcome to American Airlines, where getting there is half the fun. For English, press one. Para hablar en Espanol, numero dos.

(Eurydice presses one.)

For bankruptcy claims, press one. For oversold flights, press two. For sexual harrassment by the steward, press three. For trashed, drenched, and mutilated luggage, press four. For all other miserable complaints, press five.

(Eurydice quickly presses five.)

We're sorry. All of our representatives are currently helping other customers. Please stay on the line, and listen to bad music. Your call is very important to us.

(Bad music plays. Eurydice shakes the phone in frustration.)

EURYDICE

If it's so damned important, then answer the goddamned phone.

PHONE VOICE

Did you swear at me?

EURYDICE

No, just talking to myself.

PHONE VOICE

Then how can I help you?

EURYDICE

I'm told you have a plane leaving for Tampa in a few hours, Flight 376. But it's full.

PHONE VOICE

Let me see. Yes, we do have a single seat left on Flight 376. Do you want it?

EURYDICE

Please!!!

PHONE VOICE

Name?

EURYDICE

Eurydice Watson.

PHONE VOICE

Credit card number?

EURYDICE

Yes, it's American Express 55603-80589-3012890.

PHONE VOICE

Expires?

EURYDICE

[She cites the day of the performance.]

PHONE VOICE

That's today.

EURYDICE

Today?!!!

PHONE VOICE

You expire today.

EURYDICE

But it's still valid.

PHONE VOICE

Not after today. Let me read this back to you.

EURYDICE

Please don't bother. Just ticket me. I'm going to be late.

PHONE VOICE

All right, you have one seat on Flight 346 to Tampa, Florida, leaving at 2:45 PM this afternoon and arriving at 1:45 PM this afternoon.

EURYDICE

Wait a minute. How can the plane arrive before it leaves?

PHONE VOICE

That's just what it says here.

EURYDICE

That it leaves at 2:45 PM and arrives at 1:45 PM?

PHONE VOICE

Maybe there's a time change?

EURYDICE

(Beginning to lose it.)

The plane is going to Florida for Christ sake and leaving from Boston. How can there be a time change?

PHONE VOICE

Oh, I see the problem. That plane has been diverted to Kuala Lumpur, Malaysia. It arrives at 1:45 PM the next day. I knew there was a time change.

EURYDICE

What about Tampa.

PHONE VOICE

All our Tampa flights have been temporarily rerouted today to Kuala Lumpur, Malaysia.

EURYDICE

What do I have to do to get to Florida today? Please help me? My daughter is having a baby!

PHONE VOICE

Go to the reservation desk.

(And she hangs up.)

(Eurydice wanders back to the AA attendant.)

ATTENDANT

Any luck?

EURYDICE

No, all the flights to Tampa have been temporarily rerouted to Kuala Lumpur, Malaysia.

ATTENDANT

Listen, I've been looking at the schedules, and your best bet is this new low fare airline at Terminal X called the Limbo Liner. They have regular flights to all the southern cities.

EURYDICE

I didn't know there was a Terminal X.

ATTENDANT

At the very extreme end of the airport.

EURYDICE

(At the very end of her rope)

You've been very kind.

ATTENDANT

No problem.

EURYDICE

(Wheels her carry-on round and round in circles until the Attendant changes the name tag to "Limbo Airlines: It's Worth the Wait.")

ATTENDANT

Hello, we've been waiting for you. Welcome to Limbo Airlines: Home of the Limboliner.

EURYDICE

Do you have a goddamn seat on a goddamn flight to goddamn Tampa.

ATTENDANT

Yes, we do happen to have a goddamn seat, on the all-new luxury 787 Limboliner.

EURYDICE

Thank God.

ATTENDANT

But that flight has been delayed indefinitely, due to turbulence and flatulence.

EURYDICE

Oh, this is hell.

ATTENDANT

No, this is Limbo. For Hell, you must go to Pluto Airlines at Terminal Z, and board the River Styx Puddle Jumper. The equipment is very old, and the airline is experiencing interminable delays. But Captain Charon and his capable crew will eventually get you safely to Hell, or wherever your final destination may be. Until your flight is called, however, feel free to wait as long as necessary in Limbo's comfortable departure lounge, where time, we assure you, will pass very very slowly.

[Slow fade on Eurydice in total despair, crying "Help!!!"]

4

Sex for a Change

(An operating room. Patient on an operating table, under anesthesia, with a tag on his toe. Female nurse waiting for the doctor. After a moment he enters in his scrubs, holding up his washed hands.)

DOCTOR

Good afternoon, Nurse, what's on the menu today?

NURSE

Appendectomy.

DOCTOR

Really? I was told it was a sex change.

NURSE

Could be the wrong O.R.

DOCTOR

Could be the wrong patient. Check out his chart.

NURSE

He has no chart.

DOCTOR

(Irritated)

Well, then, read his wrist bracelet.

NURSE

(Squinting)

Caravelle. Club Med. Guadaloupe.

DOCTOR

That accounts for the flushed complexion and the bloated abdomen. But it doesn't explain why he's lying anaesthetized on an operating table. What's that on his toe tag?

NURSE

(Reading one side)

"Drastic reduction."

(Reading the other)

"Everything must go."

DOCTOR

Just as I thought. It's a sex change. Scalpel please.

NURSE

(Handing him the instrument)

Shouldn't we call Receiving first?

DOCTOR

Forceps. What for?

NURSE

This patient's HMO may not cover genital confirmation surgery.

DOCTOR

Thingamajiggy.

(She hands him a clamp.)

What the hell is genital confirmation surgery?

(He drops a round object into a bucket.)

NURSE

A sex change.

DOCTOR

Well, if it's not covered, the patient pays the hospital, who pays the surgeon, and I'm richer by a thousand shares of Microsoft.

(He drops another round object into the bucket.)

NURSE

I thought Microsoft was in a dive.

DOCTOR

Google then. Here's the HMO Expense Manual. Look up Fees for Surgical Services. It's right under my broker's phone number.

(Takes a book out of the pocket of his scrubs and throws it to her, and continues operating)

NURSE

According to this, health plans only cover sex changes for government employees in certain areas of Northern California, where the procedure is called a salpingo-oophorectomy, or a bilateral salpingo-oophorectomy if both ovaries and tubes are removed.

DOCTOR

We can't do a bilateral salpingo-oophorectomy. Our patient is—or was—a male.

(One longer object is dropped in the bucket.)

NURSE

(Checking the manual)

The males are being offered feminizing genitalplasty. But the only patients eligible for this procedure are firefighters in the city of San Francisco.

DOCTOR

As I see it, we either fly this patient out to San Francisco, register him as a fireman, and charge the city government for a thousand shares of Microsoft—er, make that Amazon—or we operate here and have him transfer the fee directly into my broker's account. What's the limit on the San Francisco insurance?

NURSE

Up to $50,000 if the surgery involves penile inversion vaginaplasty.

DOCTOR

What the hell is penile inversion vaginaplasty??

NURSE

(Reading the manual)

A procedure that turns the skin of the penis inside out and uses it for a vaginal cavity.

DOCTOR

Very creative. Let's do that one. And if the HMO rejects his application, he's in a perfect position to go and fuck himself.

NURSE

(Hesitant)

Pardon me, Doctor, but are you absolutely certain you have the proper authorization for this procedure? The Medical Board could make waves if you undertook an expensive surgical operation without appropriate clearance. Why not give the patient an appendectomy and tell him it's a vaginaplasty?

DOCTOR

Why not give him a vaginaplasty and tell them it's an appendectomy? That way we could keep the Medical Board out of the loop entirely without invading their customary coma.

NURSE

I hesitate to mention this, Doctor, but you seem unusually eager to proceed with this surgery. Is vaginaplasty a speciality of yours?

DOCTOR

Nope. This will be my virgin voyage.

NURSE

Excuse me, Doctor, but professional ethics oblige me to observe that your decision might be a little problematic.

DOCTOR

How so?

NURSE

I mean, even under the best of circumstances, like when the surgeon is trained and qualified, and might even have some experience with the procedure, there's no guarantee of absolute success.

DOCTOR

And how would you define "absolute success"?

NURSE

Aside from persuading the HMO to pay the hospital bill and the doctor's fee, I would say that absolute success is defined by the patient's total satisfaction with his new circumstances.

DOCTOR

Well, then, Nurse, you see before you a shining example of absolute success.

(Turning proudly in a complete circle)

NURSE

You?

DOCTOR

(Nodding)

I had the procedure performed on me last year. In this very hospital.

NURSE

(Amazed)

No kidding! Who was your surgeon?

DOCTOR

Jimmy Levinson.

NURSE

Not *Jenny* Levinson?

DOCTOR

No, Jimmy Levinson.

NURSE
Formerly Jimmy. He operated on herself just three weeks ago.

DOCTOR
And you know him . . .

NURSE
. . . her . . .

DOCTOR
—on a first name basis?

NURSE
He operated on me last Christmas before he became she.

DOCTOR
You are transgender, too, then?

NURSE
We prefer to say "transwoman."

DOCTOR
I thought your face was familiar. Weren't you that hunky attendant with the big biceps that used to hang out in Dispensary?

NURSE
That was me. Abe Teitelbaum in Radiology.

DOCTOR
And I was Rose Lafferty in Gynecology.

NURSE
The famous Doctor Rosie! I thought I recognized you.

DOCTOR

The obstetrical surgeon with the cobra tattoo on her shoulder.

NURSE

I loved that tattoo! I always had a kind of crush on you except you were a woman.

DOCTOR

And I always had a kind of crush on you except you were a man.

NURSE

Think of it, under other circumstances, you could have been Abie's Irish Rose.

DOCTOR

What do you mean other circumstances? These are those other circumstances.

NURSE

By God, you're right. These are those other circumstances.

DOCTOR

And what is your newly gendered name, Abe?

NURSE

Guinevere Teitelbaum, R. N. And yours, Rosie?

DOCTOR

Lancelot Lafferty, M.D.

NURSE

Lancelot and Guinevere. I believe we are a match.

DOCTOR

One last question, Nurse Teitelbaum. And your answer is very important to me. Are you a virgin?

NURSE

(Delighted with herself)

Two days after my vaginaplasty, Dr. Levinson offered me a hymenectomy as a bonus. I am as pure as the driven snow.

DOCTOR

My virginal Nurse Guinevere!

NURSE

My virile Doctor Lancelot!

(They embrace passionately.)

PATIENT

(Rising from the table in an anesthetic daze, speaking with a high voice)

Is the operation over? Are my tonsils out yet?

(Blackout)

5

Kosher Kop

(Heavy traffic sounds. A car–it should be represented by a chair–is seen on stage, carrying a middle-aged man with a briefcase. He should seem to be driving, while eating a sandwich, until we hear a police siren, and the Man brings the car to a stop. He sits frozen in his seat. A uniformed State Trooper lumbers on and stands by his car window, carrying a flashlight, which he shines in all corners of the car.)

MAN

Officer.

OFFICER

Just a minute.

(Shines the light in the man's face. The Man tries to avoid the direct glare.)

License and registration, please.

(Man hands it over.)

I see you live in Brookline.

MAN

Yes.

OFFICER

(Reading)

Joseph Mandelbaum. Jewish?

MANDELBAUM

(Muttering)

Yes. Does that make any difference? Was I speeding?

OFFICER

Please step out of the vehicle, sir.

MANDELBAUM

I thought the speed limit on the Pike was 65. I was under 60.

(Officer places him over the car with his hands and body on the hood.)

OFFICER

That's right. You wasn't speeding.

MAN

Then why stop me?

OFFICER

You wasn't speeding. But you may have been feeding.

(By now he is beginning to assume a pronounced Yiddish accent.)

MANDELBAUM

Feeding?

OFFICER

(The Officer pats him down and looks in the car. Pulls out a cheeseburger with bacon.)

Aha!

(Picks it open and brandishes the bacon)

I thought you said you was a Jew?

MANDELBAUM

Why would you doubt it?

OFFICER

THIS!

MANDELBAUM

You mean my lunch?

OFFICER

Not any more it ain't.

MANDELBAUM

You are impounding my lunch?

OFFICER

Let's just say I am collecting evidence. Pretty conclusive, I'd say. A cheeseburger with bacon? Who eats such goy dreck.

MANDELBAUM

What do you mean?

OFFICER

First of all, mixing dairy and meat is a shanda, strictly forbidden. And bacon is the product of an unclean animal.

(Starts writing on a piece of paper)

MANDELBAUM

You're giving me a speeding ticket for eating non-kosher food?

OFFICER

Who said a speeding ticket. I'm giving you a feeding ticket!

MANDELBAUM

Arresting me for eating?

OFFICER

I'm not arresting you. I am arestauranting you! This meal ticket represents a 20% discount on any dish you want when presented with this menu.

(Hands him a menu)

A bargain. Soup to nuts. Glatt Kosher. For you special.

MANDELBAUM

What restaurant?

OFFICER

A brand new Brookline dairy restaurant opening today, right across from Kupel's, called *Milka Dich und Fresse Dich*. Free parking. Easily accessible on the Green Line. Here. Check out the prix fixe.

MANDELBAUM

What kind of police officer promotes a new dairy restaurant?

OFFICER

I'm not a police officer. I'm a press officer. It is my job by any means necessary to fill the seats with Jewish tushies.

MANDELBAUM

(Impatient now)

So you're a flack for an eating establishment? Who gave you the right to get all gussied up like a State trooper?

OFFICER

I told you I was a press officer. This is my press uniform, newly pressed.

MANDELBAUM

What's *your* name,

(Ironic emphasis)

Officer?

OFFICER

Chaim Peretz. Choose your order. I'm in a big hurry. I've got to chase down five more customers before I go home tonight and watch the Jewish Channel.

MANDELBAUM

I could have you arrested, you know, Peretz. For impersonating a police officer.

PERETZ

(Blushing)

I was that good?

MANDELBAUM

Actually, you were lousy. Your Yiddish accent ultimately gave you away.

PERETZ

That was a character choice.

MANDELBAUM

It doesn't come naturally?

PERETZ

I can do all the accents. English. German. Swedish. Beyelorussian:

(Gives him a few samples)

English: "All right now, matie. Out of the vehicle. We got a little infraction here." German: "*Raus* from the car, *augenblicks sheisskopf.*" Swedish: "Withdraw from the automobile. I vant to be alone." After only two years of drama school yet. Do you want to hear my showcase piece? A man meets an old Rabbi in the woods who says to him, "Go no further—there is a dangerous Bacon Tree down the road." The man shrugs this off and runs smack into a tribe of Indians. Screaming he tells the Rabbi: "I got scalped down there by Indians and all you warned me about was a Bacon Tree." "Oy, my English," says the Rabbi, "What I really meant, it was a Ham Bush."

MANDELBAUM

(Getting involved in the menu)

I'm not interested in your acting career, Peretz, or your bad jokes either. But I am getting hungry. Let's see what *Milka Dich und Fresse Dich* has to offer. 20% off anything on the prix fixe, you say? Hmm, I'd go for the blintzes. If I wasn't on a diet.

PERETZ

A diet you shouldn't worry. These are blintzes that float like a feather. Topped with yoghurt light instead of heavy sour cream.

MANDELBAUM

What kind of a Kosher restaurant serves the customer reduced fat food?

PERETZ

The Jews have suffered throughout history from persecution, discrimination, extermination. We should have to suffer chronic heartburn, too? *Milka Dich und Fresse Dich* is dedicated to dietary change, which is why we have been accredited as a gas-free, non-*greps* establishment.

MANDELBAUM

So you got no egg creams?

PERETZ

Are you crazy? You want us to lose our license? Of course, we got egg creams, and Fanta Grape and Hire's Root Beer and Doctor Pepper too. Just because we're modern don't mean we're non-traditional.

MANDELBAUM

One question. Is the staff too courteous? I wouldn't want to eat at a Kosher establishment where I didn't get insulted every ten minutes by irritable waiters. It would ruin your reputation, not to mention my appetite.

PERETZ

What are you talking? We have a full four-month training program for waiters. They are not allowed to graduate until they have learned how to insult you the minute you walk through the door. And you won't see a single one of our waiters he hasn't got his thumb in your matzoh ball soup.

MANDELBAUM

My kind of place.

PERETZ
So you are close to making a decision?

MANDELBAUM
Don't rush me, Peretz. These things take time. And I have miles to go before I eat.

(Looking dreamily at the audience)

And I have miles to go before I eat.

(During these speeches, Peretz has been scratching his behind.)

MANDELBAUM
What's the matter, Peretz, you got hemerrhoids?

PERETZ
Mr. Mandelbaum, if you see it on the prix fixe menu, we got it. Otherwise, go *a la carte* with the schmaltz herring.

MANDELBAUM
All right, give me the fried kishkes and boiled cabbage.

PERETZ
Mr. Mandelbaum, it's not for you.

MANDELBAUM
It's not for me? How come, Peretz?

PERETZ
It's not for you because you're a crank

(He pronounces this krenk.)

MANDELBAUM
Peretz, youre calling me a "crank"?

PERETZ

No, Mr. Mandelbaum, I don't mean what you mean a "crank." I mean it's not for you because you're *particular*.

MANDELBAUM

All right, give me the chicken soup with matzoh balls . . .

PERETZ

(Into his radiophone)

One order *knaidlock*, comin' up . . .

MANDELBAUM

Followed by a slice of cheese cake and a cup of coffee.

PERETZ

A dose of heartburn and a cup of acid indigestion on the way.

MANDELBAUM

And no speeding ticket, right?

PERETZ

No, only a feeding ticket.

(Rips off the page)

For you, 25% off. You know why? Because you're a crank– And I mean that in the Yiddish sense, namely that you're very very *particular*.

(He munches hungrily on Mandelbaum's cheese-burger with bacon.)

(Lights)

6

Allies in Blunderland

(A table set under a tree. Starched Hair and the Mad Hater throwing teacups at each other.)

Enter Sarah, dressed as Alice.

THE MAD HATER

Who are you? Get lost. There's no room for illegal immigrants at this Tea Party!

SARAH

My name is Sarah and I'm 150% American. You must be the Mad Hatter, though you look an awful lot like Bill O'Reilly.

THE MAD HATER

I'm not the Mad Hatter. I'm the Mad Hater. And there's no room at the table for people of your kind!

SARAH

Isn't this Wonderland?

THE MAD HATER

No, silly. Wonderland is over on the left bank of nowhere. This is Blunderland.

SARAH

If you're the Mad Hatter . . .

MAD HATER

(Interrupting)

Hater!

SARAH

(Taking no notice)

. . . then I guess your friend must be the March Hare, though he looks an awful lot like Donald Trump.

STARCHED HAIR

My name is Starched Hair, okay? And I say, You're fired.

SARAH

I am? But I was never hired.

STARCHED HAIR

All right, then, you're hired, and fired, and off with your head! Okay?

SARAH

Hmmm. Off with your head! Isn't that the campaign motto of the Red Queen?

THE MAD HATER

There's no room here for Reds or queens.

STARCHED HAIR

Or any other kind of illegal immigrants. No room, no room! You're fired!

SARAH

Where I hail from, we got room for every full-blooded American! Oceans of seawater. Gallons of oil. Drill, baby, drill.

THE MAD HATER

Silence. I'm the only one here allowed to rant and rave. This is a quiet retreat.

SARAH

Never retreat. Advance! Reload!

STARCHED HAIR

Now you're talking Second Amendment language I can understand. Here, have a cup of tea. Right?

SARAH

(Eagerly pouring)

You betcha!

THE MAD HATER

You betcha! Now I know who you are. The hockey mom who draws cross hairs over Commie aliens who support health care reform.

SARAH

Cross hairs?! That's a blood libel.

THE MAD HATER

What's a blood libel?

SARAH

The red smears I get from the liberal press.

STARCHED HAIR

So you never drew cross hairs over the faces of your political enemies?

SARAH

They wasn't cross hairs, they was surveyor symbols.

THE MAD HATER

I think I got enough savvy to tell a gun sight from a home site. And they was cross hairs!

SARAH

Surveyor symbols!

STARCHED HAIR

What's wrong with gun sights?

(Patriotic background music)

A well-regulated militia being necessary to a free state, the people have a God-given right to draw cross hairs and shoot immigrants. Also to grope vaginas. When I become Groper-in-Chief, everyone will be permitted to do anything they want.

SARAH

Not with me.

STARCHED HAIR

Why not? This is a Tea Party, not a nunnery.

SARAH

I am totally opposed to stripping, petting, smooching, necking, cheating, teen-age pregnancy, abortion, same-sex marriage, and any other kind of hanky-panky.

THE MAD HATER

So what kind of action *do* you prefer?

SARAH

Total abstinence.

STARCHED HAIR

I haven't tested that particular position yet, though I've done all the others. Look at the size of my hands.

SARAH

It's not a sexual position, it's a moral position. As they say, abstinence makes the heart grow fonder.

THE MAD HATER

And your moral position is to replace the cross hairs on the M16s of our brave boys in uniform with surveyor symbols.

SARAH

Surveyor symbols are very accurate within a thousand feet of the target.

STARCHED HAIR

And the target being surveyed?

SARAH

Every liberal in our sacred nation, from Anchorage to Fairbanks.

THE MAD HATER

And what about Hawaii?

STARCHED HAIR

Hawaii? I knew you was an illegal immigrant, okay? When are you going to pay for that wall?

SARAH

I'm talking about Alaska, now, not Mexico! The pure American landscape. Porpoises. Caribou. Oil rigs. Refineries.

THE MAD HATER

Now I got ya. Welcome to Blunderland! There's always a place for dunderheads like you at our Tea Party.

SARAH

People got no right to say I'm a dunderhead just because I don't whine or cuss, and look at some things different.

STARCHED HAIR

Take your seat at the table. You're obviously as mad as we are.

(She sits down.)

SARAH

The table is laid for a great many more.

STARCHED HAIR

We're expecting a great many more.

(Pause)

Your hair needs starching.

SARAH

You should learn not to make rude personal remarks about my hair. Leave that to the liberal press.

STARCHED HAIR

The liberal press needs starching, too.

THE MAD HATER

Now here's a question. Why did you say that our Muslim President should refudiate the Grand Mosque on Ground

Zero? What did you mean when you said that you'd misunderestimated him?

SARAH

I admit I wee-weed up the language a bit there. But remember, Shakespeare also liked to invent new words.

STARCHED HAIR

Who's Shakespeare?

SARAH

A speechwriter for English kings.

STARCHED HAIR

Another illegal immigrant. He's fired! And so are his kings! And so are you!

THE MAD HATER

No, Sarah is welcome to Blunderland. You have my personal permission to tickle Starched Hair.

SARAH

(Tickling his hair)

So fun. And you can join me any time for a tour of Sarah's Alaska.

STARCHED HAIR

Like Obama's Hawaii. Not a part of America!

SARAH

The highest part. I can even see Russia from my third floor window.

(Looking at The Mad Hater's watch)

What a funny watch. It tells the day of the month, but doesn't say what time it is.

THE MAD HATER

Yes, because it's always tea time in Blunderland.

SARAH

So that's the reason for all those teacups on the table.

STARCHED HAIR

That, and because we've got no illegal Mexican immigrants around to wash the dishes and clean the toilets.

MAD HATER

Then we'll have to move to somewhere else.

STARCHED HAIR

Exactly.

SARAH

Where?

STARCHED HAIR

To that bigger Blunderland in the District of Columbia. Do you think you're ready for that?

SARAH

My voices tell me God has a mission for me there.

THE MAD HATER

What mission?

SARAH

To start another Tea Party.

STARCHED HAIR

Not in my administration.

SARAH

I would never presume to know God's will or speak God's words. But the good Lord has told me to abolish health care, zero social security, dissolve trade unions, stamp out planned parenthood, and criminalize gay and premarital sex, meanwhile keeping a close eye on Russia from my third floor window.

STARCHED HAIR

Okay, you're not fired, because you're a real homegrown patriot with your own personal arsenal, Okay? I may make you my Vice-President if I don't take that job myself.

THE MAD HATER

Pack up the tea things and stow them in the bunker. We're moving this Blunderland Tea Party to the White House.

STARCHED HAIR

Immediately.

THE MAD HATER

Indubitably.

STARCHED HAIR

Inevitably.

SARAH

I getcha! You betcha! Great to have metcha!

(They embrace.)

(Blackout)

7

The Comfort Zone

(A room. Totally unfurnished, except for a gleaming white toilet in the middle of the stage. Two windows. Sounds of explosions and occasional gunfire outside. Two Uzi automatic rifles against the wall. Pete, with a manual in hand, and his wife Sally are on stage contemplating the toilet with awed reverence.)

SALLY

Fantastic.

PETE

Amazing.

SALLY

Elegance itself. What does it do, besides the obvious?

PETE

Read the manual.

SALLY

You read it.

PETE

It's hard. My left eye won't open.

SALLY

(Concerned)

Still bleeding?

PETE

Probably a damaged duct. Tear gas affects the blood flow.

SALLY

Well, comfort yourself with our newest purchase.

PETE

Read me the specs.

SALLY

(Reading)

The cyclone flushing system can be operated by remote or sensor control.

PETE

What a wonder.

SALLY

Front and rear warm water injections with pressure variations.

(Deep satisfaction)

So it doubles as a bidet.

(Reading)

The seat is heated by temperature control.

PETE

Or would be if we had any power.

SALLY

Power? We don't even have plumbing.

PETE

They'll turn the water on as soon as they retake the State House.

PETE

But what's the sense of advanced technology without the means to use it.

SALLY

Have patience. Things will settle down soon.

(An enormous explosion nearby rattles the room. Sally and Pete run to pick up their rifles.)

PETE

Where did that come from?

SALLY

(Looking out of the window)

Starbucks. Look, it's in total ruins. Must have been some explosives stashed in that SUV on Charles street.

PETE

I bet there's a ton of casualties.

SALLY

Fifteen dead. Sixty-seven wounded.

PETE

How do you know?

SALLY

It's the figures they always quote after a bombing. The Occupiers used that coffee house as their downtown headquarters.

PETE

(Back to the toilet)

What else can this thing do?

SALLY

(Back with the manual)

Flushes and refills—faster than normal, of course. And the toilet seat opens and closes by remote control.

PETE

Yes, but that requires power, too.

SALLY

Maybe it could work on batteries.

PETE

Do we have any left?

SALLY

Only the ones in the flashlight.

PETE

I still can't believe the guy wouldn't stick around long enough to connect the damned thing.

SALLY

When you're selling contraband goods, you don't provide installation services. Besides, where would he ever find closet bolts and plumber's putty?

PETE

Yeah, but to just plunk the damned thing down in the middle of the floor like that, and run—

SALLY

Well, his truck was under fire.

PETE

So all we got here is a piece of sculpture.

SALLY

Seems so.

PETE

Form without function.

SALLY

Some day we'll get it going.

PETE

A work of art called Useless Crapper.

SALLY

The Japanese are so way ahead of us.

PETE

Well, they're not in the middle of an uprising.

(Sounds of gunfire in the street. Pete and Sally recover their Uzis and start shooting out of two different windows.)

PETE

Goddamn Special Forces. I thought they had secured the area around the State House.

SALLY

Most of them have defected to the Tea Party Militia.

PETE

And the National Guard? What's their excuse?

SALLY

The National Guard is only reserved for emergencies.

PETE

You don't call this an emergency? With the Tea Party shooting everybody in sight and the Occupiers squatting in every public space on the Hill?

SALLY

Where else could they go?

PETE

What's wrong with the Common?

SALLY

Too exposed. This is not the Arab Spring, it's the Boston Winter. After all that rain and snow, it's too damp to sleep in tents.

(She's got a bead on a target outside.)

PETE

Why don't the Occupiers squat in the Ritz or the Four Seasons?

SALLY

Wrong image.

(She shoots.)

There! I got one.

PETE

Occupier or Tea Partier?

SALLY

Dces it matter? Our mission is to survive.

PETE

So that makes how many today?

SALLY

Thirteen. Not counting the wounded.

PETE

I got no way to beat your record.

SALLY

You had a pretty good week in January.

PETE

You mean the Fedex van? That wasn't my doing, that was an improvised explosive device.

SALLY

Which you triggered with a single shot. Awesome!

PETE

Rattled our windows.

SALLY

Lit up the sky.

PETE

An Aurora Borealis.

(Sally hugs him.)

SALLY

We still have our amusements.

PETE

We still have our pastimes.

SALLY

I admit I miss the good old days when you could walk down Boylston Street without getting a bullet through your neck. Fairs. Parades. Street parties.

PETE

Vandalism. Muggings.

SALLY

Still, it's wrong to romanticize the past. We got a lot of advantages now we never dreamt of then.

PETE

Name one.

SALLY

Well, how about this toilet?

PETE

It is a beauty.

SALLY

Not a scratch or stain or mark on any surface.

PETE

Well, it is brand new.

SALLY

I think the secret of happiness is learning how to live with things you got rather than longing for things beyond your reach.

PETE

One of the reasons I always loved you, Sally. Your wisdom. You're a wise woman.

SALLY

But I still wonder: Was it worth all that money?

PETE

What else would we do with the cash? Fly down to Puerto Escondido for a holiday? All the airports are closed. Buy a new condo? Most of the streets are levelled. Visit the Mall? All the luxury shops are shuttered.

SALLY

You can't live without food.

PETER

There's still lots of groceries around. Have you forgotten already? You just have to wait until midnight when the militia's asleep and the armed guards have left Whole Foods for the day and the night watchman has fallen into a drunken stupor. Who needs credit cards when you can jimmy open the revolving door with a good crowbar.

SALLY

Especially when the currency is so inflated.

PETE

So be glad I saw that toilet guy cruising the street, looking for a customer.

SALLY

And offering a good deal.

PETE

Half the price off.

SALLY

I apologize for complaining, Pete. The toilet was a brilliant buy.

(A shot through the window wounds Sally in the arm. She falls to the floor, screaming. Pete starts shooting out of her window.)

PETE

Goddamn bitch bastards.

(While shooting)

Sally, you all right?

SALLY

My arm is busted.

PETE

I'm tossing the grenade.

(Goes over to the corner and picks up a hand grenade; throws it out of the window. Big explosion)

That'll show those fuckers!

SALLY

Good.

PETE

It's our last grenade.

SALLY

How many rounds we got left?

PETE

I'd say about fifty. How's your arm?

SALLY

Must have been a rubber bullet. Didn't penetrate the skin. Put a plaster on it, would you?

(Pete gently leads her over to the toilet.)

PETE

Here, hon, come over here and sit. It'll be a comfort to you.

(He begins to apply a large Band-Aid to her arm.)

SALLY

It's always a comfort to be near something beautiful.

PETE

Any pain?

SALLY

Just some throbbing. And your eye?

PETE

A little better.

SALLY

Is your vision good enough to read the manual to me?

PETE

I still got one good eye. "The cyclone flushing system can be operated by remote or sensor control."

SALLY

So cool.

PETE

"Front and rear warm water washing with intermittent temperature controls."

SALLY

I love you, Pete.

(He puts his arms around her as he reads further in the manual.)

PETE

"Heated seat with alternating intensity."

SALLY

Such a comfort.

(The lights dim and go to black, as the sound of gunfire is heard offstage.)

(Blackout)

8

Gun Play

Scene: The Teller's window of a local bank in Tombstone, Arizona. A well-dressed man walks up to the window, where the teller is counting cash, puts a pistol to his forehead, and speaks:

ROBBER

Hand over your cashbox. This is a holdup.

TELLER

(The Teller takes out a revolver and puts it to the robber's forehead.)

Hand over your pistol. This is a showdown.

ROBBER

You a cop?

TELLER

Yep.

ROBBER

So what's a pig like you doing behind a Tombstone bank window pretending to be a teller.

TELLER

And what's a thug like you doing behind a loaded gun, pretending to be a robber?

ROBBER

You first.

TELLER

Usually, I'm behind a Tombstone school door, pretending to be a security officer. But the kids are off on spring break.

ROBBER

And usually I'm in a Tombstone office building, pretending to be a rental agent. But there's no condos left on the market.

TELLER

So that's why you come here with a loaded pistol and try to hold up a bank?

ROBBER

I'm also a charter member of the National Rifle Association.

TELLER

They need money?

ROBBER

We're collecting enough cash to buy a hundred assault weapons.

TELLER

And for what purpose, may I ask?

ROBBER

To exercise the constitutional rights of a well-regulated militia.

TELLER

To hold up banks?

ROBBER

To occupy the Halls of Congress if any gun haters try to ban our weapons.

TELLER

Which gun haters?

ROBBER

Obama and his gang of Communists.

TELLER

Your weapon, please.

ROBBER

I have a license for this thing. It's against the law to expropriate a privately-owned hand gun.

TELLER

Not if you bring it into a savings bank for criminal purposes.

ROBBER

I am one of 4.3 million dues-paying, card-carrying members of the NRA, which means I have the sacred right to carry weapons into any public area as long as I have a license.

TELLER

I thought the NRA was primarily made up of hunters.

ROBBER

That's right.

TELLER

So what are you hunting in the Tombstone National Bank? Goldfish? Sand Dollars?

ROBBER

We also hunt bad guys.

TELLER

I don't see any of those types around here. Except maybe you.

ROBBER

Me? I'm a good guy.

TELLER

And how would you define a bad guy?

ROBBER

Anyone who wants to ban guns. Our Chairman, Wayne LaPierre, says that the only way to prevent armed violence is for all the good guys to shoot all the bad guys.

TELLER

So that's why you're brandishing—what's that you're brandishing?

ROBBER

A magazine-loaded compact semi-automatic Smith & Wesson .45 ACP Chief's Special.

TELLER

So that's why you're brandishing a magazine-loaded compact semi-automatic Smith & Wesson .45 ACP Chief's Special—to hunt for bad guys?

ROBBER

And for looters, perpetrators, and white-tailed deer. What kind of weapon are you brandishing?

TELLER

A Smith and Wesson Compact 9 millimeter. Now why don't you lower your weapon, and I'll put down mine and then we can discuss this issue calmly like rational gun owners.

ROBBER

Okay.

ROBBER

(Laying down his weapon on the counter)

Thank you for showing some respect for my sacred Constitutional rights.

TELLER

And thank you for showing some respect for the law. You don't have a sacred Constitutional right to rob a bank.

ROBBER

Maybe not, but the Second Amendment gives me the right to overthrow an unjust government.

TELLER

Where does it say that?

ROBBER

(Reciting by rote)

"A well regulated militia being necessary to the security of a free state, the right of the people to keep and bear arms shall not be infringed."

TELLER

You've completely misunderstood that clause.

ROBBER

(Startled)

What do you mean?

TELLER

It's in error. The Supreme Court will soon be arguing a case that says the Second Amendment has nothing to do with guns.

ROBBER

(Incredulous)

"The right to bear arms?"

TELLER

It's a misspelling. The Constitution doesn't guarantee the right to "b-e-a-r" arms, so men can walk about freely carrying weapons, but rather the right to "b-a-r-e" "arms," so women can walk about freely wearing short sleeve jerseys.

ROBBER

Then it's not about shooters . . . ?

TELLER

No, it's about hooters.

ROBBER

You're kidding me. Why should a well-regulated militia be concerned with female flesh?

TELLER

How else can a militia remain well-regulated?

ROBBER

Well, until the Supreme Court decides on this case, it will still remain legal for me to keep my arms bare—I mean, keep and bear arms—in defense of my Constitutional rights.

TELLER

Not if it results in the murder of innocent bystanders by people with violent psychiatric disorders.

ROBBER

You think I'm a psycho?

TELLER

You're sure behaving like one.

ROBBER

Then arrest my mother. She let me play with video games as a kid.

TELLER

Video games don't kill people. Guns kill people.

ROBBER

No, people kill guns. Read Wayne LaPierre.

TELLER

What are you talking about?

ROBBER

Our Chairman, Wayne LaPierre, says that the Liberal-Socialist pussies are trying to abolish the weapons that protect us against the bad guys.

TELLER

Yes, because guns kill people.

ROBBER

No, people kill people unless the good guys bear arms against the bad guys. The state of Arizona, which has twenty percent more automatic weapons per capita than anywhere else in the world, has 6.3% less murders.

TELLER

Actually, you got that wrong. It has 6.3% *more* murders.

ROBBER

Where did you that statistic from?

TELLER

From certified police records.

ROBBER

Communist propaganda.

TELLER

Look, we can't stand here with loaded guns pointed at each other's heads. Why don't we holster our weapons, and debate the issue over a stein of beer?

ROBBER

Okay, so long as you don't turn into a bad guy and try to arrest me. Otherwise, I would be obliged to exercise my Constitutional rights and put a bullet through your brain.

TELLER

Well, you haven't committed a crime yet, only attempted one, and I'm the only witness. So let's go to the local bar and look at some bare arms.

ROBBER

Sounds good to me. What's this place called?

TELLER

The O.K. Corral.

ROBBER

(Enthusiastic)

Shoot! Okay with me!!

TELLER

By the way, what's your name?

ROBBER

Billy Clanton. And yours?

TELLER

Wyatt Earp.

ROBBER

Well, dang me! I know all your brothers. Why don't you bring them along?

TELLER

Great! And you can bring all yours.

(They shake.)

(Blackout)

9

The Press Assess the Gettysburg Address

(Situation Room music. A television studio, with the two commentators, Sean Inanity and Greta Insufferable, sitting around a table, with the moderator, Wolf Spritzer.)

WOLF

Hello, I'm Wolf Spritzer in the Simulation Room, welcoming you back to your favorite news program, NCN, the Nitpick Cable News. We once again interrupt our six month coverage of missing Malaysian Flight 370 and EgyptAir Flight whatever to briefly comment on the President's Gettysburg Address this afternoon. Joining our discussion once again are Greta Insufferable and Sean Inanity. Hello, Greta and Sean.

GRETA

Hi, Wolf. Thanks for having me on the program.

SEAN

Yeah, thanks a bunch.

WOLF

Let's start by listening to the President's concluding remarks.

We hear the final phrases of the Gettysburg address being spoken by Abraham Lincoln, while three TV pundits prepare their comments on the event.

VOICE

and that government of the people, by the people, for the people, shall not perish from the earth.

WOLF

Sean? Greta? I think our whole television audience is itching to hear your commentary–

SEAN

It was okay.

GRETA

B– over C+.

WOLF

Am I right in concluding that neither of you thinks the President added anything new to the national debate?

GRETA

I don't say the guy isn't a sharp operator, Wolf. But what did he hope to accomplish by dragging the press corps all the way down to a remote whistle stop in Pennsylvania just to listen to a few morbid paragraphs about dead veterans?

SEAN

You know what I think? He was trying to bring closure to an awkward campaign issue.

WOLF

Which one?

SEAN

The Civil War. It's not exactly a very popular issue with American voters.

WOLF

Certainly not in Mississippi.

GRETA

It doesn't have much clout in the Capitol either. But hold up your commentary on the speech for a minute. I'm more interested in the motives behind the speech.

WOLF

And your take on that, Greta?

GRETA

Transparently political. He was wooing undecided voters.

SEAN

Who? Dead soldiers?

GRETA

No, not soldiers who can't shoot bullets but voters who can't cast ballots. The President wasn't just talking to tombstones. He was addressing all the living relatives of the dead.

SEAN

And how big a constituency is that? I'd say the President was more likely directing his remarks to the Editor of Bartlett's Familiar Quotations. Look at his opening phrase: "Four score and seven years ago." Now how many people use fancy language like that any more? Why didn't he just say "It's been eighty seven years" like any other average American Joe Sixpack?

GRETA

Pure showboating. Designed for sound bites. And the most transparent one was this–

(Looking in her transcript)

–"the world will little note, nor long remember, what we say here." Really? Then why invite the entire press corps? Formal invitations, bearing the White House seal.

WOLF

Are you suggesting that our President is a headline hunter?

SEAN

No doubt about it, Wolf, a motive he hides through fake modesty.

(Quoting)

"The world will little note nor long remember what we say here." Hello? Every word out of his mouth is meant to be long remembered, and endlessly quoted on every front page, cable channel, blog, tweet, and eighth grade essay.

WOLF

Let's turn to some of the substantive issues the President brought up this afternoon. What do you think of his claim that all men are created equal. Greta?

GRETA

Well, the most obvious omission is his failure to mention women. Why? They don't have the vote.

SEAN

To me, all this talk about equality only exposes the alien nature of Lincoln's Socialist thinking.

WOLF

Really? You think the President is a Socialist?

SEAN

You're bound to pick up subversive ideas when you weren't born in this country.

WOLF

Abraham Lincoln wasn't born in this country?

SEAN

He's an illegal immigrant from Africa. How else do you explain those bushy eyebrows and that swarthy dark skin? The guy claims to be from Kentucky but has anyone ever seen his birth certificate?

GRETA

Isn't Abraham a Jewish name?

SEAN

I don't know what part of Africa he comes from. But you can bet your bottom dollar that all this socialist garbage about equality is designed to take hard-earned money away from real red-blooded American one-percenters. I consider that alone sufficient grounds for impeachment.

WOLF

Let's be fair. He said that all men were created equal, not that all men were entitled to equal income.

SEAN

If you make an argument for equal birth, then you are making an argument for equal income.

WOLF

But if he's really such a subversive, how do you explain the fact that he always wears a top hat and a tailcoat!

SEAN

A disguise. He dresses like a Wall Street banker in order to con the super PAC committees into bankrolling his election campaigns.

GRETA

Sean, you mentioned his complexion and his eyebrows. You know what worries me more? His beard. Can you imagine how much it costs the taxpayers to trim a growth like that every day?

SEAN

John Edwards's haircuts cost the citizens of North Carolina $500 a month.

WOLF

Well, there's not enough time remaining tonight to resolve the equality issue, or the socialism issue, or the birther issue, or even the barber issue, for that matter. So before we return to our coverage of Malaysian Flight 370, I'd like to devote the remaining moments of the discussion to what may prove to be the most controversial issue in the whole speech—his reference to a "government by the people, for the people, and of the people."

GRETA

Yeah, which people . . . ?

SEAN

You mean government on the *backs* of the people—!

WOLF

Whoa, there, Sean, Greta. Let's be fair. Maybe he does mean what he says about government being about the people. He did free the slaves, didn't he? They didn't have the vote.

GRETA

They will when the Emancipation Proclamation kicks in. Every ex-slave will become an American citizen—on welfare.

SEAN

That's why we need redistricting. That's why we need people like Sheldon Adelson and the Koch brothers. To support any politician who opposes increasing welfare taxes.

WOLF

What's the worry? Does anyone think there might be a black President in America's future?

GRETA

I'll bet we see a black president before we see a female president.

SEAN

A black president of the United States? You must be dreaming.

WOLF

Well, we certainly won't be seeing one soon.

(Listening to his earpiece)

I'm told we're running out of time. Any final thoughts before we return to our coverage of missing airline Malaysian Airline 370?

SEAN

I agree the President's speech had a few quotable phrases. But it was pure rabble-rousing. Too much babbling, too much muckraking. That's what happens when you try to hide your radical politics under bloated language.

GRETA

I would criticize the President for making his speech in such a remote part of Pennsylvania on such a wet day. Especially when nobody bothered to supply the press corps with umbrellas.

SEAN

Well, as the saying goes, you can fool some of the people all of the time, and all of the people some of the time. But you can't fool all of the people all of the time.

WOLF

Didn't Lincoln say that?

GRETA

Who?

WOLF

Well, whoever said it, we have to wrap things up now. I want to thank these two distinguished commentators for being here tonight, and for lending their expertise to such an historic event. Greta Insufferable? Sean Inanity? Come back soon.

GRETA

Thanks for having us.

SEAN

Yeah, thanks a bunch.

WOLF

What's next for you guys?

GRETA

I'm going to the White House next week to interview the First Lady about her marital problems. There's a rumor the President was overheard in their bedroom shouting "Damn you, Mary Todd!"

SEAN

I'll be covering Lincoln's visit to a new British comedy called *Our American Cousin* at Ford's Theatre in Washington.

WOLF

I saw it in London. What an explosive hit! I'm glad they're giving that play a shot in front of Lincoln at Ford's. Greta Insufferable, Sean Inanity, on behalf of our viewers, I want to thank you both for joining the best political team on television. Keep up your informed, insightful work. Viewers, we welcome your opinions about the President's speech. Just call 1-800-693-CARP, or write to us care of the Bitch and Bellyache Division of NCN, your Nitpick Cable News. Now back to a few more hours covering that lost Malaysian airliner.

(He shakes hands with the two commentators.)

(Blackout)

10

Moses and the Deep Red Sea

NARRATOR

One day in ancient Egypt, around the last week in April, a Jewish family produced a son named Moses. Around the same time of the month a Druzish family produced a daughter named Zipporah. Zipporah grew up healthy and beautiful, but Egyptians enjoyed killing Jewish babies like Moses, and Pharaoh had ordered midwives to stop helping Jewish women give birth.

PHARAOH

No more surrogate mothers.

MIDWIFE

Okay, Pharaoh.

NARRATOR

So Moses' mother, Jochebed, had an idea.

JOCHEBED

Let's put these sweet little cuties in a basket, drop them in the Nile, and pretend they're Egyptian. Someone will save them. (I hope.)

NARRATOR

And guess what! At that very moment, Pharaoh's daughter, Batya, happened to be walking by the riverside, thinking about what gown she wanted her Daddy to buy her for the Senior Prom.

BATYA

What's this? A baby in the river. In a cute Nikki's basket. I think I'll take them home.

NARRATOR

She took the Moses baby home, changed its diapers, fed and reared it, even though some people always suspected the baby was really hers.

One day, when he was all grown up, Moses was walking by the river, getting a little tan, when he ran into this older woman—his real sister, Miriam.

MIRIAM

You look just like a brother I once had. In fact, you are the brother I once had. Isn't your name Moses?

MOSES

How did you know?

MIRIAM

Because you've got that rare belly button thing, known as an outie.

MOSES

It's a wise child that knows her own brother, but it's an even wiser child who knows her own brother's belly button.

MIRIAM

And you know what else? You're Jewish. You can be bar-mitzvahed.

MOSES

Wow! Does that mean I get to receive useless presents like initialed handkerchiefs?

NARRATOR

Moses visits the Pyramids and sees hieroglyphics of Pharaoh ordering Jews to be drowned in the river. The next day he comes upon an Egyptian whipping a Jewish slave. He slays the man and runs away to the desert. There he sees a beautiful young girl named Zipporah.

MOSES

Let me help you draw some water from the well.

ZIPPORAH

Why, thank you. My, you got big muscles.

MALE MOSES

You think I got big muscles?

ZIPPORAHS

And smart, too.

MOSES

Let's get married.

ZIPPORAHS

Why not? But I'd better introduce you to my father, Jethro, first.

JETHRO

Why are you bringing this goy into my house?

ZIPPORAH

Because he brought me water from the well. And also he just offered to marry me.

JETHRO

I've got seven children to get off my hands, so I like that offer. But he's not Jewish, is he?

MOSES

I have a weakness for pickled herring and rude waiters.

JETHRO

Well, there must be Jewish blood somewhere.

NARRATOR

Zipporah and Moses got married, and had two sons, Gershon and Eliezer. But God was angry with Zipporah.

GOD

Anyone born in your house better be circumcised, or I'll kill them.

ZIPPORAHS

(Terrified)

I don't have a kitchen knife.

GOD

Try this broken rock.

NARRATOR

And she circumcised Gershon and Eliezer with the sharp stone, and touched Moses' feet with it.

ZIPPORAHS

Now you are a husband of blood.

MOSES

Great. But what's that smell?

ZIPPORAHS

What smell?

MOSES

Ashes! It's a burning bush.

BURNING BUSH

Hi, Moses. Will you guys do me and yourselves a big favor?

MOSES

It's a talking burning bush.

BURNING BUSH

Go to the Pharaoh and tell him, "Let my people go."

ZIPPORAH

Anything for a burning bush.

GOD

Actually, my name is God. A burning bush is just one of my numbers. I also do a pillar of fire. And if you ask me nicely, I can do great thunder. Now go to this wicked Pharaoh and tell him "Let my people go." And try not to sing it in that fake African-American basso. Let him know something nasty is going to happen.

MOSES

Watch me.

(To the Pharaoh)

Hey, Pharaoh, you'd better let our people go, or you're going to get some really disgusting plagues.

PHARAOH

Oh yeah? Like what?

GOD

Like blood, frogs, mice, wild animals, toenail fungus, dirty fingernails, pimples, hemorrhoids, heartburn, and smelly armpits.

PHARAOH

Who cares.

GOD

Let the plagues begin. Ending with the death of all Egyptian first-born.

PHARAOH

All right, get rid of the Jews. Chase them into the Red Sea. It's only borscht anyway.

NARRATOR

The Jews are chased into the Red Sea. But God raises his staff and, lo, the seas part.

SCARED LITTLE GIRL

I'm a scared little girl.

RED SEA

Don't be frightened. I'm parting my sea so you Jews can get to the other side.

MOSES

What's on the other side?

RED SEA

Saudi Arabia.

MOSES

And that's an improvement?

GOD

You don't like it? Then wander in the desert for forty years, and you can forget about entering the Promised Land.

MOSES

Forty years is a long time.

GOD

Just a few years longer than a Seder. Where you wait for hours for the matzo ball soup.

THE OTHER JEWS

We're waiting.

GOD

And gefilte fish.

OTHER JEWS

It's coming?

GOD

And bitter herbs.

OTHER JEWS

Oy!

MIRIAM

Sing the praise of God for saving us from the Egyptians, the Red Sea, and clogged-up ears.

ALL

Hosanna. Hosanna. Hosanna.

ZIPPORAH

A hose on a what? This story is already too full of cold water.

GOD

I think it's too full of hot air.

Curtain

III

Commendatory Word Plays

1

Wendy Wasserstein

As I type the letters of Wendy's name while composing these memorial remarks about her, I am wracked with pangs of memory and remorse. Wendy was part of that extraordinary coven of Yale Drama students in the mid-1970s that included Chris Durang, Meryl Streep, Ken Howard, Steve Rowe, Lewis Black, Sigourney Weaver, David Epstein, and Albert Innaurato, among many gifted people who may forgive me for leaving them out. Unlike her more confident classmates, Wendy always looked as if she wanted to put her head under her wing and disappear. Wendy's unusual modesty, linked to her famous shyness, and her even more legendary generosity of spirit, were always constants, even when she became a celebrated writer for the New York stage, and a witty contributor to *The New Yorker*, the *Times*, and other periodicals.

She wrote *Uncommon Women and Others*, a play about her Mount Holyoke days, for her MFA degree in 1976, and it was produced the next year at the Phoenix Theatre in New York, where Meryl got her start after Yale as well. I regret that I was not enthusiastic enough about this play when she was a student to produce it on the Rep's main stage, though her work in the cabaret was always delicious—particularly a satire she and Chris Durang wrote with the immortal title

"When Dinah Shore Ruled the Earth." (I pirated that title in a recent essay of my own called "When Dramaturgs Ruled the Earth.")

I held back at the Rep on Wendy's play for the very reason I so admired her character. Her sense of humor was a delight, but it lacked acid, I thought, the kind of edge that cuts to the quick. And while she always had truly serious things to say, I believed her themes were aereated a bit too much with her bubbling charm, intoxicating sweetness, and sparkling wit, always admirable in their ambition, but perhaps too light in their execution. In those post-Vietnam War days, we thought we needed radical surgery, not goodnatured satire, to lance the cankers of the time.

That may have been the reason why the Rep in the 1970s was featuring the plays of Chris Durang and Albert Innaurato, notably *The Vietnamization of New Jersey*, *Benno Blimpie*, and *The Idiots Karamazov*, while Wendy's work was being done in the Annex or the Cabaret. But even in future years, when she was dazzling New York and winning Pulitzer Prizes and producing such popular hits as *The Heidi Chronicles* and *The Sisters Rosenzweig*, some imp of the perverse still prevented me from fully endorsing her plays. If Wendy sensed my reservations, she never seemed to resent them. She was always unfailingly warm and generous toward me and my theaters, never missing a Gala or an award ceremony as a show of her support.

With her last produced work, *Third* at Lincoln Center, I was finally able to see that Wendy was a major American playwright, and before writing my review for *The New Republic*, I sent her an email saying just that:

> Just got out of your play. Your very best—brave, complicated, clarifying, illuminating, and very very moving (Doreen cried all the way home). You alone in your

> generation have bitten off this very important subject, and handled it in the most balanced manner, avoiding both moral correctness and political correctness in favor of a courageous capacity to live with doubts and ambiguities. Very Keatsian. Warm congratulations. You should feel very proud. Hope you are well and enjoying your grand success. Much love, Bob.

I was very happy to see Wendy writing at full strength and relieved to be in a position, finally, to give one of her plays my full enthusiastic endorsement. But to my surprise, because Wendy always replied promptly, I didn't hear from her until two weeks later, when she sent me an email saying, "I'm sorry it's taken me so long to respond, I have been away. I was so touched by your email and am very grateful for your words." Only when I called Chris Durang to check on rumors that Wendy was sick, did I learn exactly what was meant by that hidden phrase "I have been away." She had contracted lymphoma and was having massive doses of chemotherapy that later sent her into shock. A few weeks later she was dead.

To Wendy's family, I want to say how deeply all of us share your grief over the death of this uncommon woman. I want to assure little Lucy that she will find much comfort in the coming years as she rediscovers her mother's sweet loving nature in the conduct of her plays and her playful conduct, the written and unwritten memories she has imprinted on us all. I want to say I share with all her friends their sense of desolation and loss over Wendy's horribly premature death. This shy, good, and modest artist will always be etched indelibly in our memories and in our hearts (2006).

2

Austin Pendleton

I am very happy that the New Repertory Theatre has chosen to honor Austin Pendleton because Austin Pendleton is an artist whom so many of us honor in our hearts. A complete man of the theater, he has functioned as actor, director, teacher, playwright, and general creative inspiration. His moving play, *Orson's Shadow*, about another complete man of the theater, Orson Welles, has continued to reverberate in my mind since it opened in New York in 2005, after its premiere at Steppenwolf five years earlier.

Austin played in a lot of Hollywood's funniest movies, including *Catch-22* and *What's Up, Doc?*, and also, believe it or not, as Motel in the original version of *Fiddler on the Roof*, the only one in the show, according to recent scholarship, to survive a nervous breakdown at the hands of Jerome Robbins.

I had the deep personal satisfaction of having Austin as the director of the final play in my Shakespeare Trilogy, *The Last Will*, at the Abingdon Theatre. He also played the leading role as a sad, aging victim of paranoia, though he was unable to join us in China when the play was invited to the Wuzhen Festival.

Austin Pendleton is hardly an unsung hero of the theater, but I think we ought to sing his praises as often and as loudly as we can. He is one of the few American theater artists who have maintained total integrity, dignity, and good nature throughout a long and meritorious career (2016).

3

Justin Kaplan

It is always wrenching to talk about the passing of a gifted friend, especially when the humane values of our deteriorating culture seem to be one of the few defenses left against selfishness and corruption. Tonight is particularly wrenching as we pause to memorialize the passing of that gentle giant, Justin Kaplan, familiarly known as Joe. He was the very opposite of an average Joe, indeed a large man in every sense of the size. As a biographer, he covered almost the whole spectrum of nineteenth-century literary lights—Walt Whitman, Lincoln Steffens, and particularly Mark Twain about whom he wrote two definitive books, not to mention a defense against stupid politically correct attacks on the so-called racism of *Huckleberry Finn*.

A proud Jew, he was nevertheless madly in love with nineteenth-century American culture. His last book was entitled *When the Astors Owned New York: Bluebloods and Grand Hotels in a Gilded Age*, possibly a secret attempt to get a good room in a posh hotel at a reduced rate. But Joe loved all forms of literature, because he was a lover of language. He became the editor of the sixteenth and seventeenth editions of Bartlett's *Familiar Quotations*, updating them with his own self-declared prejudices, his own delicious feeling for the politically absurd. Criticized for including only four citations by Ronald Reagan, he replied that he had done the president a big favor. He limited President Clinton only to three, climaxing with his immortal remark to the Grand Jury in the Monica Lewinsky impeachment: "It depends on the meaning of what the word 'is' is. If the—if he—if 'is' means is and never has been, that is not, that is one thing. If it means there is none, that was a completely true statement," which must be the most incoherent quotation in all of Bartlett's, though from one of America's most articulate men.

With his gifted wife and occasional collaborator, Anne Bernays, Joe wrote a splendid book called *The Language of Names* about the etymology of our proper names, and he was involved in another unfinished collaboration with her before his death.

The oddest story about Joe Kaplan, considering his gentle nature, concerns the time when, after being hospitalized for pneumonia, he developed what is called "hospital delirium," striking a nurse and threatening to kill his beloved wife and daughter in what was perhaps the only violent moment of his entire life. What fictional world was he feverishly inhabiting then?

Joe was a faithful reader of obituaries. In one of his editions of Bartlett's, he quoted Woody Allen's remark (I am tempted to call it Woody's deathless remark) to the effect that "It's not that I'm afraid to die. I just don't want to be there when it happens." Justin Kaplan was very much there when it happened. But oh, how all of us wish that it hadn't happened and that he was still with us, here (2014).

4

Jonathan Miller

How does one begin to describe Jonathan Miller and all that he has meant to the various theater institutions he has informed with his wisdom and expertise?

My image is of a solid, imperturbable pillar of calm, though I remember once in the early days of the ART when he almost put his fist through a wall in a justifiable fit of frustration. He was my student in Technical Direction at the Yale Drama School and served with the Yale Rep under Rob Orchard before we all departed for Cambridge. But even in his student days, he was a paternal figure, supervising and fathering all those under his watch. And, of course, along with the family he fathered in the theater, he has been the father of two glorious children, Abigail and Ben, while being happily married to Ellen, the lovely and loving wife who gave birth to them.

Jon has always been among those who allow others to take the credit while he does the hard work. Symbolic of this condition, I have always thought, was the fact that he shared his name with the brilliant British theater and opera director, Jonathan Miller. No one ever suspected our Jon Miller of starring in *Beyond the Fringe*.

But he has been a bright star throughout all these years, providing the illumination with which many great talents have been able to do their work. So hail to Jonathan Miller and everything he represents. The art of the stage would not exist without people of his modesty and selflessness (2009).

5

Blushing

(Response to a speech by Mike Wallace introducing me into the Hall of Fame)

What my friend Mike Wallace is trying to tell you, and he should know, is that if you manage to live long enough, people will forgive you anything. Imagine it, the Hall of Fame! Before tonight, the closest I ever came to a Hall of Fame was in 1945 when I was a deck cadet in the Merchant Marine and my shipmates inducted me, hitherto a virgin, into a hall of infamy in Panama City. Some of you might suspect my interest in legitimate theater dates from that fateful encounter. Certainly prostitutes and theater people have been confused with each other ever since Shakespeare's days, possibly because they both get paid for giving pleasure. About how many professions is it possible to say that today?

Actually, my theater career began at the age of five when my parents sent me to elocution school ("erocution school") to correct a lazy ("razy") "L" and a case of lip lethargy ("rip rethargy"). That's what drama schools were called in those days—elocution schools—to distinguish them, I suppose, from houses of ill-fame. While curing my "l" problem, my teacher, June Justice, put me on stage to play the part of Little Boy Blue. The next day she dressed me in a pirate's costume, painted a moustache on my lip, and made me recite a short poem. (I still remember the lines: "I make fair maidens walk the plank and little children I beat and spank.") That was the beginning of a lifelong passion—for acting roles (not spanking children). Those without the good fortune to be born without a speech impediment had to develop an interest in the arts through the school system—which is why it is essential that these programs be restored, or we will no longer have any artists or audiences left at all.

It is customary on these occasions to say that this honor really belongs to someone else. In my case that's literally true. I don't mean God or my agent (I've seen no evidence of the former and have never been signed of one of the latter). I am referring to the countless good people with whom I have worked and lived during my fifty-two-year association with the four nonprofit theater companies I helped to found. I don't have time to name all these admirable people in three minutes or even three hours. But let me try to mention some of the most important to me, aside from my beloved wife and family.

Chief among them are the countless theater artists to whom I owe whatever reputation has brought me to this Hall of Fame. I have had my time on stage as an actor, director, playwright, adaptor, critic, and educator. But, though this may sound like false modesty, my major function, indeed my greatest pleasure, has been to facilitate and develop the talents of others, particularly the members of the Yale Repertory and American Repertory Theatres, and my students at the Yale Drama School and the ART Institute for Advanced Theatre Training. It is both to that external family as well as to my more immediate family that I dedicate this honor with gratitude and love. Thank you. (2009).

6

Lewis Black

It is my distinct pleasure to welcome Lewis Black to Suffolk's Modern Theatre, probably the tiniest house he has played since his twenties in the West Bank Cafe.

Lewis is not only one of my favorite people and a former actor at the ART, he is a Yale Drama School student from the early 1970s, which means that even though he hated the school we share a lot of loves, particularly old friends.

I use the word "old" advisedly, because now that Lewis has passed sixty he thinks he's turned venerable, and talks a lot about memory loss.

That may be why his name is in the title of most of his concerts—*Stark Raving Black*, *Lewis Black Unleashed*, *Basic Black*. So he won't forget it. I'm only in my eighties, but I generally have to consult my heating bills to remember mine.

These concerts, let me add, along with his frequent appearances on *The Daily Show* with Jon Stewart and his outrageous biography, *Nothing's Sacred*, have established Lewis Black as the outstanding stand-up comic of our time. And it didn't come the easy way. As he says, he had to lick his way up every rung on the ladder.

A combination of Lenny Bruce and Freddy Nietzsche, George Carlin and Karl Marx, Richard Pryor and Edward

R. Murrow, he has managed to create a new artistic form—stand-up Theatre of the Absurd. As George Carlin once said, "Lewis has it all—brains, balls, and chops." He is at the same time a fearless political commentator, a relentlessly obscene philosopher, a dauntless playwright, an explosive comedian, an unapologetic consumer of pot and junk food, and an ongoing candidate for apoplexy.

His rage is that of a warm-hearted if disaffected student of humanity, who probably thinks both of our political parties should be annihilated. But it makes him the perfect spokesman for all the angry, dispirited Americans (they're becoming a majority) who believe that our country has been stolen from us by its meanest, greediest, most hypocritical citizens.

If there were a God, I would thank him for Lewis Black. If Lewis Black is correct in believing that God has been stolen, too, let's just thank this atheist Jew for being back and being Lewis Black (2016).

7

Mark Rylance

Mark Rylance is that rare, consummate artist who not only works in all three media—theater, film, and television—but who has established his supremacy in all three as well. Consider his Oscar-winning performance in *The Bridge of Spies*, his Tony-Award Winning Performance in *Twelfth Night*, and his Emmy-Award Winning Performance in *Wolf Hall*, to name but three of his manifold awards. He is presently the finest actor in the English-speaking world.

But the profession owes a lot more to Mark Rylance than performance awards. He is an artist who has helped raise the condition and the reputation of the actor to a new height. As artistic director of the Globe in England for ten years, he demonstrated that great theatrical art is not created by stars but rather by a family that works together over a long period of time and that shares the same values and ideals.

I had the great good fortune to have Mark as a member of our family at the American Repertory Theatre in its 1991–92 season, playing the back-to-back roles of *Hamlet* and Hamlet's later incarnation Konstantin Treplev in Chekhov's *The Seagull*. Both were performed in repertory under the direction of our resident director, Ron Daniels. Mark played Hamlet in pajamas and the results were dazzling. What was equally dazzling was Mark's modesty and seriousness and the way he adapted himself to the needs of our permanent resident company.

It is always a pleasure to pay tribute to a great actor. But it is a special pleasure to honor an actor who raises the stature of the entire theater profession. That is why I am so proud to offer the 2016 Robert Brustein Award to this brilliant man (2016).

8

Todd London

Todd London's new book *Open Call* is an elaboration and extension of his three classic essays in *American Theatre Magazine* in 1995, a deeply felt rumination on the hopes, triumphs, and disappointments of the American actor.

Todd achieves his insights by following, for a year-and-a-half, the careers of fifteen graduates of the 1995 class of the American Repertory Theatre Institute where he was a key inspiration for a number of years, adding an epilogue examining the status of the same actors twenty years later. The result is both heartwarming and heartbreaking.

In his various positions, among them director of New Dramatists, literary director of the American Repertory Theatre, and (currently) executive director of the University of Washington School of Drama, Todd London has demonstrated a passionate belief in the actor's capacity to transform our spirits, as well as her or his own, by a commitment to the ideal of repertory theater company work.

This, indeed, was also the theater ideal animating the ART, the acronym of a permanent company of actors, many of them engaged in training students at its institute for the same kind of future. The student could perform under student directors, or professionals, either in the Experimental or Cabaret Theatre or on the Main Stage. As I have probably boasted too often, when the theater was at Yale, Meryl Streep played most of the leading female roles at the Rep when still a student in her third year. Indeed, when the theater moved from Yale to Harvard in 1979, its regular members (among them Jeremy Geidt, Carmen de Lavallade, Christopher Lloyd, Cherry Jones, John Bottoms, Tom Hill, and Max Wright, and others) were joined by the entire graduating class of 1979 (among them Mark-Linn Baker, Marianne Owen, Harry Murphy, Stephen Rowe, Rick Elice, and others).

I mention these names not only to celebrate the quality of the talents being attracted to the training programs, but also to show that for a special period of our history actors were genuinely attracted to resident company work.

Todd London's interviews with the fifteen members of the 1995 class demonstrate that this attraction, alas, could rarely be sustained and that a society that celebrated selfish individualism would hardly be very supportive of resident company work. Todd learns that most of the actors whose lives he examined (a major exception being Randall Jaynes, an early member of Blue Man Group, and still with them to this day) were being jostled away from the nonprofit theater, beckoned into an uncertain future of profit and celebrity. The goal of a regular if modest income, a companionate family relationship, and the capacity to grow as an artist was being lost in a culture of self-advancement.

As for the writer himself, the book inadvertently reveals that if some theater people may sometimes disappoint our hopes and expectations for them, very occasionally someone comes along to restore our faith in the whole process. Todd London is a rich example of that hope. He writes with a profound sense of compassion and humanity and a strong feeling for history. He is one of the great success stories of the not-for-profit resident theater, and deserves our gratitude and applause. His words help make plays the joyful experiences they always promise to be (2016).

9

Robert Kiley

When we lost Bob Kiley, we lost a true and noble man. Our hearts go out to his devoted wife, Rona, and his loyal sons, Ben and David.

Dedicated to public service, Bob committed his life to helping people navigate through difficult pathways. And I use the travel metaphor deliberately because most of Bob's life had to do with moving people through crowded cities. He was also a CEO of various companies—as well as a CIA agent in the days when those letters were an honorable abbreviation. And he was chairman of many boards, as well as the first chairman of the American Repertory Theatre.

I remember vividly the time when the American Repertory Theatre first came to Cambridge from New Haven, and some people, repelled by the radical approach, were clamoring to have it and me shut down. I turned to Bob and asked what I should do, and I have never forgotten his answer: "Stick to your religion." Most other board chairmen would have advised me to compromise or resign.

Bob certainly stuck to his own religion, which was to clean up the local transit systems. This he did literally in Boston and New York where he had all the graffiti scrubbed off subway cars that had previously looked more like action paintings than public transit vehicles. He did the same cleanup for the London Underground and London Transit and, if left unchecked, would probably have improved systems in Europe, Asia, Iceland, and Alaska as well.

He was dedicated to making people move easily through life. To adapt W. B. Yeats' tribute to Jonathan Swift:

> Imitate him if you dare, world besotted traveller,
> He served human mobility.

Coda

The title of this book deliberately emphasizes the verbal importance of words in plays. For I mean the title to be taken not only literally, but figuratively as well. At the same time, a theatrical piece has opposing meanings—as both a work and a play, which has its own significance as well.

The theater is the only artistic medium where opposites such as work and play are used to signify the same object. You may have to work to understand good theater, but good theater should have its playful side as well.

I am one who has always believed that the theater should be taken seriously, on a scale with literature, classical music, and fine arts. But to take the theater seriously, you must also be prepared to enjoy it, not only as work but also as play. If this book has tickled your funny bone as well as touched your mind, then it will have fulfilled its central purpose. Thank you for taking this patient journey with me.

Index